SAGEBRUSH

To

SHAKESPEARE

By
CARROL B. HOWE

First Edition 1984

Table of Contents

ABOUT THIS BOOK -

This book is about events and people. From the first elephant-hunting migrants from Asia, who established a frontier on the lakes and rivers, to those who faced an economic or cultural frontier. Most of the people had a strong impact on the events that took place. The events, in turn, left a lasting effect upon the heritage of those living to-day.

One of the purposes is to describe the way things were during the various formative periods in our history. The main reason it is written, however, is to be sure that the achievements and contributions made by the people described are not forgotten.

This is not intended as an objective biography of any of them. Much of it is written in the first person. You cannot work with, for, and around people for years, without forming attachments and feelings that destroy an objective appraisal.

This is not a parade of saints. We can be thankful that many of these people were stubborn as mules or they would not have achieved the things they did. Most were seeking security and profit but these were secondary to long term goals.

I am greatly indebted to those whose names appear in the list of sources at the end of the book, also to those whose names appear in the text. Without the help of families, many pictures could not be published.

I am also indebted to Nora Rock, Ron Poole and Anne Howe for art work; to Eleanor Brown of the Siskiyou County Museum for help; and to Charles Kemp of the Shaw Historical Library who gave both help and encouragement. Most of all I am indebted to my wife Marjorie for transcribing my illegible, scribbling into English, then typing the manuscript.

THE LAND, LAKES AND MOUNTAINS

The year is 1922: I am a passenger in the back seat of a model T touring car. Beside me and under me, are some of the necessities for a camping outfit - tents, bedrolls, pans and groceries. Sleeping bags and Coleman stoves had not yet been invented.

In the front seat was my cousin, Si, the driver, and his father, my Uncle Frank. Frank Howe was the nearest to being a frontiersman in our family. He was a cook for the army party that had first surveyed and taken soundings in Crater Lake in 1888.

In another model T car behind us was a party made up of my brother Harry, father J. B. Howe, George Howe of Albany and Dee Cowshow who was later to become mayor of Brownsville.

After leaving Ashland, our Fords ground grudgingly over the old Greensprings Road. We stopped occasionally to add water to a sometimes boiling radiator. The steep grade of the old graveled Greensprings Road made it necessary to drive the model T in low gear. This was done by pushing a pedal with the left foot. Much of the time going uphill our drivers had to hold down on the low gear pedal.

Our main destination was Crater Lake but another purpose of the trip was to visit my brother, Cecil. He was working as a bridge carpenter for the Southern Pacific Company. They were constructing a new railroad line to be called the "Natron Cutoff" from Klamath to Eugene. Cecil's address was Kirk, Oregon.

The trip down the east side of the Cascades seemed uneventful but as we broke out of the pine trees and crossed the river at Keno, I can still remember my vivid impression of the Klamath country: abundant water, great distances, sagebrush. It was truly different. This lasting impression of the Klamath country makes it easy for me to understand the reaction of the Applegate Party when they first gazed at this same view on July 4, 1846. Lindsay Applegate wrote: "At noon we came into a glade where there were water and grass and from where we could see the Klamath River. After noon we moved down through an immense forest, principally of yellow pine, to the river and on about six miles. All at once we came out in full view of the Klamath country, extending eastward as far as eye could reach. It was an exciting moment after many days spent in dense forests and among the mountains. The whole party broke forth in a cheer."

As our Ford touring safari motored up the main street of Klamath Falls, I was impressed by the large Elks Temple building. We did not stay long in Klamath Falls after obtaining gasoline and proceeded along the Klamath Lake's edge, then made camp near a clear cold ditch south and east of the town of Fort Klamath. Our camp cooks soon had a fire going in a little pine grove where we learned of the feeding habits and persistence of Klamath County mosquitoes.

As a lazy twelve year old boy, my principal job was gathering firewood and occasionally doing dishes. This was the longest trip in my life. I drank in the frontier stories of one uncle and listened carefully to the explanations of another who was a frontier scientist and scholar. No thought was given to the idea that destiny might bring me back to this beautiful and fascinating country.

It is not easy to describe what is meant by the term Klamath country. Early explorers called it "Land of the Lakes." Culturally and historically, it includes areas that might not fit in geographically.

The miners of Yreka, California, and the miners of Jacksonville, Oregon, played an important part in its history. Names like Gazelle and Shaniko crop up in the commerce of the region. The first telegraph line went from Jacksonville to Fort Klamath. The Ashland area served the fruit-hungry settlers from the Silver Lake and Tule Lake basins.

The Southern Oregon College and the Shakespearean Theater have contributed heavily to the educational and cultural needs of the Klamath residents.

The prehistoric people of Nevada and Lake County provided the roots and foundation of the Klamath, Modoc and Paiute Indian people. Lakeview later became the governmental seat of the Oregon side of the line.

The economic and cultural ties of northern California are still so close that people on both sides of the state line proudly refer to the "State of Jefferson."

Geographically, the parts of the Klamath country are very different. On the west the high Cascade Range formed a barrier during the millions of years that hot liquid lavas flowed intermittently to form a high plateau of lava and basalt. Layer upon layer, this formed the hard deep crust that underlies Klamath County.

The new plate tectonic geology tells us that later gigantic and indescribable movement of the continental plates within the earth caused these deep lava formations to break up and pull apart. Their scarp faces can be traced all along the southern part of Klamath County east into Lake County, northern California and through the states of Nevada, Utah, Arizona, forming what is called the Range and Basin Province.

As these faulted blocks of stone broke up, normally along a north and south line, some were pushed up creating high rims; some slid down in great faults. The friction of the slippage in some cases created such heat that the rocks and soils were fused in smooth surfaces called

2

MT. STUKEL SLICKENSIDE —A rock quarry near the west point of Stukel Mountain has exposed a slickenside very near Hill Road. The lower part of the picture shows the mixture of dirt and broken rock called talus. This has eroded from the mountain above and rolled down. Above the talus, the lighter smooth surface of the slickenside is exposed. Above this, juniper trees on the upthrust mountain can be seen. There is no way of knowing how deep into the earth the slickenside extends.

MT. STUKEL FAULT—The works of man such as railroad cuts, highway cuts and quarries often reveal geologic features that have been covered by the elements of time. This small fault is exposed in the rock quarry on the side of Mt. Stukel. The small fault shows how the stratum marked A has been separated by the fault line.

3

STRATIFIED MOUNTAIN SIDE—The highway 97 cut on Spring Creek hill north of Collier Park reveals how a former marsh was forced upward by the force of tectonic plates. The black layer of peat is now near the top of the mountain. Layers of volcanic ash, diatomite, basalt and pumice reveal the history of the mountain.

slickensides. The low basins which later filled with soil were called grabens by geologists. The high rims such as Abert Rim and Hart Mountain are called horsts.

Along the fault lines where the blocks separated, weak seams allowed the hot molten magma to meet the water from above. From this, the hot springs have formed and a valuable geothermal source of energy lies below. In the state of Nevada, where underlying rock contains minerals, the super-heated steam and water have carried valuable silver and gold into the strata above.

The Cascade Range that was a barrier to the lava flows also had a decided effect upon the climate and vegetation on the east. Westerly winds carrying moisture lose much of it in the high and cold mountain range. On the east, pine trees replace firs and oaks. Juniper and sagebrush occur on the sunny side of the faulted mountains, other species sometimes on the shady north.

The northern part of the Klamath country has been called the High Lava Plains by geologists. Much of it has been covered with a layer of volcanic ash and pumice from Mount Mazama. Since it is easi-

CRUMP GEYSER—In Lake County's Warner Valley the water filtered down to meet with hot magma underneath. A drilled well released the heated water and steam creating the Crump Geyser. Other geothermal wells can be found along the graben north of Lakeview.

WEATHERED VOLCANO—Soil has weathered away from this extinct volcano leaving the harder rocks which are now called Fort Rock. This is now a state park in Lake County, Oregon.

MT. SHASTA—The magnificent peak of Mt. Shasta can be seen well into the Sacramento Valley. Here the snow waters caught in the great altitude keep the river flowing throughout the year.

LAND OF THE BURNED OUT FIRES—This lava flow occurred only about 500 years ago when the soft molten rock issued from Fleener's Chimneys.

ly penetrated by water, the layer holds the moisture, then gradually feeds it into the springs that form the streams and lakes of the Deschutes and Klamath drainage basins.

The flat basins lying between the faulted mountains filled with water creating lakes and marshes. Over the thousands of years waterfowl adopted these wetlands for their stopping place on the spring flight south from the arctic regions. A great variety of water birds, as

CATACOMBS CAVE—It is one of the many caves in the Modoc Lava Beds National Monument. It was formed when molten lava flowed out toward Tule Lake leaving a hollow tube.

well as birds of prey, can be found on the several refuges that have been established for their protection.

The Cascade region is crowned by some of the most beautiful snow-capped mountains in the world. The mountain named "Sastise" by the Hudsons Bay Company leader, Peter Skene Ogden, casts an aura of majesty from the Sacramento Valley well into Oregon. Here, schools, irrigation districts and lodges have adopted the name Shasta. The steep west slope of Mount Shasta drops off into the gold country of the older Klamath mountain mass.

Toward the east lies a most remarkable area of volcanic activity. Medicine Lake lies in an extinct volcanic caldera and the Modoc Lava Beds National Monument to the north contains almost every variety of volcanic formations. Called "Land of the Burned Out Fires," the lava flows have formed hundreds of caves, as well as cinder cones, chimneys, natural bridges and craters.

West of the Cascades the underlying rocks contain minerals. The magic word "gold" caused the populating of regions such as Jackson County and western Siskiyou. Miners, packers and merchants quickly built the towns of Yreka and Jacksonville while the river valleys filled with competing gold seekers. Volunteers from these areas occasionally joined to protect wagon trains from attacking Indians but they returned to the west after their mission.

The east side of the Cascades, which contained no gold, was populated by a few livestock ranchers and guarded by soldiers at scattered forts.

The descendants of these soldiers, miners, stockmen, and later the timbermen, railroaders and farmers have all meshed into an economic unity to develop the resources as well as the cultural and political institutions that has given the Klamath country a tradition and attitude which is unique and different from many parts of Oregon and California.

ON THE TRAIL OF THE FIRST AMERICANS

The Creator was not in a hurry when the Klamath country was built. A mountain could be pushed up by the pressure of the tectonic plates, then immediately the forces of erosion would start the eternal process of tearing it down.

A wet weather cycle would fill the flat basin between the faulted ranges with deep water, then a dry cycle would reduce the lakes to marshes. The marshes might remain for a few centuries when lack of rainfall would eventually make them into dry playa deserts.

During the time the flat basins were filled with lakes and marshes, deposits of diatoms and peat would buildup a new stratum on the bottom. During the desert cycles, the lake residue could be blown away by dry desert winds. There are many such playa deserts in the Great Basin which, of course, includes much of the Klamath country. One of these basins at China Lake in California showed three marshy levels divided by other sediments, one above the other in the strata.

The first Americans also were not in a hurry as they moved along the steep-walled valleys. They adapted their life styles to the geographic and climatic conditions of the times. While one day was vitally important to their survival, a few centuries in the thousands of years of their occupation might bring little change. The home of these early people might simply be the site where the last large animal was killed, or a more permanent camp could be maintained at a creek, a spring or a cave.

We know they prepared the implements for the hunting of large mammals. They also used the meat, hides and bones. Recent studies have shown that ancient people led a much more varied life than was previously believed.

Archaeologist Emma Lou Davis, who studies desert cultures extensively, said, "Desert people were people of the marsh whenever marsh conditions were available----Paleo Indian campers in panamint North Basin and Paleo American camel scroungers at Lake China--all did their grocery shopping in a marsh. Why? Because a marsh supplies plant foods; bird foods; some large mammal foods, and lake-creature goods. The swamp also supplies such industrial raw materials as reeds, rushes, roots and fiber."

The finding of ancient type projectile points no longer can be taken as an indication that the maker was exclusively a hunter of large mammals. The time frame in which the first Americans lived here has also been pushed back. Sophisticated dating techniques have been applied to specimen that lead to previously unheard of antiquity.

8

MORTAR WITH QUERN—Two giant mortars each fashioned for use as a quern were excavated in land leveling by William LaVerne. They prove that ancient hunters of the Lost River Circle were utilizing vegetable materials, as well as the products of the hunt. The indentation for the quern can be seen near the bottom of the bowl.

One test of a mammoth tooth that was excavated with two sophisticated lithic (stone) flakes was found to be 42,350 years old. (Author's note: Not all scientists have accepted this and other more ancient dates as being valid.)

Windust Culture

What about the evidence of ancient people in the Klamath country? Some years back when I was giving a talk to a group in Eugene, Oregon, I commented on one group of projectile points, illustrated by a slide, that I believed to have great age. I had no evidence, just belief. Soon after, I received a request from a graduate student, John Fagan, that he be allowed to borrow the points for study. Somewhat reluctantly I agreed to send them giving an exact location of the site where they were found. Visiting the university later at his invitation, I was shown the specimens along with others he had borrowed which had been found at the same site. They showed a definite similarity and were demonstrated to be from the same Paleo Indian culture as the famous Windust Cave site in Washington.

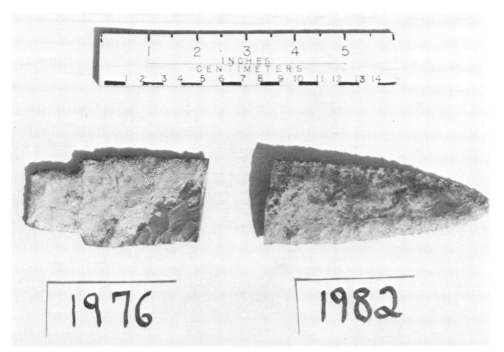

GIANT WINDUST SPEAR—Several years passed, after the shouldered base of this spear was found, before the point was exposed by erosion. It is the largest such spear every reported.

The Windust site in northern Lake County has been visited several times since the dry windy years of the 1930's. All the artifacts had been removed except for scattered bits of bone and obsidian flakes. My visits proved to have large sentimental value but in 1976 a piece of flaked obsidian showed above the surface of the blown out lake bed. It proved to be the basal end of a large point. It was shown to Dr. Melvin Aikens at the University of Oregon anthropology department. It was then brought home and placed with other Windust specimens.

In 1982 I returned to the site to show it to a friend. Neither of us found anything exciting except I did find the point from a knife or spear. Upon my return, I tried in vain to fit the point to other Windust fragments - no luck. Recently in 1984, Steve Wallman and Dewey Dietz visited me to make drawings of ancient points for a publication. I placed my assortment before them and explained that the parts did not fit. Holding the point to the shouldered base, I was astounded and elated - I had a perfect giant Windust spear! I left the room briefly and on returning found a misfit base had been placed where the good one had been. It was easy to suppress my urge to kill as both men were big strong timber fallers. Besides I liked them.

The Windust culture is, in my opinion, only one of at least four

WINDUST POINTS FROM LAKE COUNTY—The points shown above the spear were the ones which led to the identification of the ancient Indians in Lake County. Cave studies showed the culture appeared in the cave about 10,000 to 11,000 years ago. Could these ancient hunters have lived first in the Klamath country and then migrated to the Snake River Canyon?

WINDUST PHASE POINTS—Extensive research has been done by Washington State University at Windust Cave and Marmes Rock Shelter. David Rice has described the results of the study and the name Windust has been used to describe the culture. The points in this picture illustrate several of those found on a Windust site in Lake County, Oregon.

ancient cultures to be found in the Klamath country, Siskiyou, Modoc, Lake and Klamath Counties. Evidence of these cultures, except by professional archaeologists, depends upon erosion.

KILL AT MAMMOTH SPRING—Artist Nora Rock has recreated a Clovis site scene in Modoc County. The ancient hunters attack a mammoth mired in the mud. The Clovis point pictured is of white chert and was found in Lake County, Oregon.

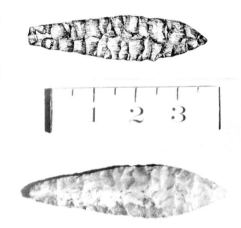

MODOC COUNTY HASKETT POINT—The first Clovis fluted point was positively identified by H. M. Wormington and other professional archaeologists in 1972. Since that time several artifacts from Clovis sites have been reported. The lancehead type point above has been named the Haskett type. The author believes this point is older than Clovis culture points.

(Drawing by Steve Wallman)

Clovis People

In Modoc County it was water and ice erosion that cut into the ancient habitations to scatter the tools of the former occupants in all directions. It was here that the first positively identified Clovis point was found. I'm sure other associated objects are from the Clovis culture but this cannot be proven until professional archaeologists can

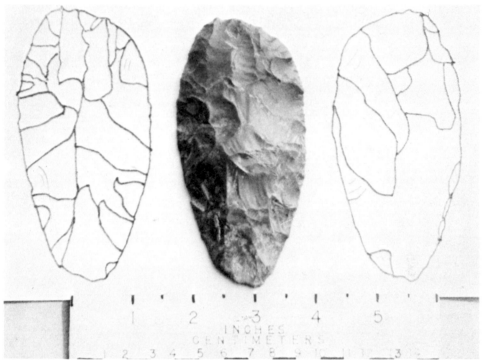

MODOC COUNTY KNIFE—This jasper uniface knife is from an ancient site in Modoc County. The flaking technique is similar to that used to make fluted points.

MODOC COUNTY—A Sandia type point of basalt and a shouldered point of brown jasper. The basalt point shows much basalt grinding.

excavate the site and establish the association. Some years ago arrangements were made to take Dr. LeRoy Johnson to the place but water levels in Clear Lake had obscured the site. It is still under deep water.

Since the first Clovis-type fluted point was found, six others have been reported and photographed. We were still not sure that the points were left by traveling bands of the big game hunters or if these famous stone workers were once permanent residents of the region.

In 1983 Dewey Dietz, an amateur collector from Redmond, dispelled any doubt. He found fragments of fluted points. Recognizing their significance, he reported the find to Dr. Fagan, who is now archaeologist for the Army Engineers. Excavations were carried out with the help of volunteers and university scientists. More than fifty parts of fluted specimens have been found. Dietz, the informed amateur, has proven that the Clovis people were in the Klamath country to stay. He deserved the honor of having the site named after him.

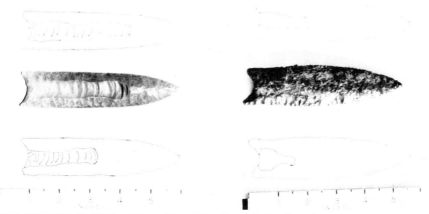

CHRISTMAS VALLEY CLOVIS—Since identification of the first fluted Clovis point in 1972, several others have been reported. These were found in northern Lake County, one by Mrs. Mary Anning, the other by Wayne Harting. Restrictive laws, accusations and harassment are making it increasingly difficult to get the valuable information that can be supplied by amateur collectors.

Camel Eaters

In Siskiyou County, the erosive force was the work of wind and the structures of man. When the railroad pushed north through the marshes adjacent to the Klamath River in 1908, the water flow which normally entered from the river into Lower Klamath Lake was cutoff. At about the same time, the few other sources from springs was partially utilized for irrigation. The lake slowly became lower until it was nearly dry. A growth of milkweed, the ranchers called Chinese lettuce, grew to produce a heavy cover over the rich black soil of the lake bed. Soon it was discovered that both sheep and cattle would thrive and fatten on the succulent milkweed plants.

Ray Laird, whose family raised cattle, said that one winter he fed no hay which was an unusual occurrence in the region. Sheepmen and

14

MERGANSER CLOVIS—This fluted point of a very dense obsidian was brought to the surface by an excavation for a drain ditch. It was found by Dr. Rodney Wright about four miles from the Midland point. The location indicates that the user probably lived on the old Henley Slough which once connected Lost River with the Klamath River.

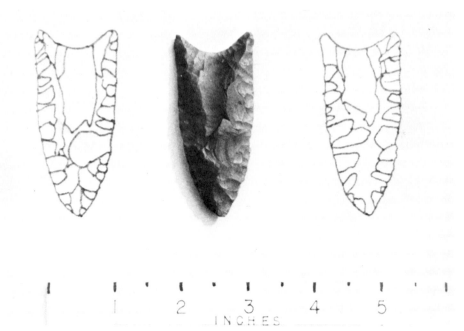

MIDLAND CLOVIS—A perfect example of the Clovis type point made of reddish brown chert was found by Dick Meeker. This is the first such point reported from the north shore of Lower Klamath Lake.

cattlemen seemed to work out satisfactory patterns of cooperation in using the government owned land. It was not until the late 1928's that the milkweed cover was completely consumed. The black peat-like soil started to blow, nearly always from the south and west. I have seen days when it seemed like twilight at 2 p.m. due to the billowing dust storms.

JAVELIN POINTS—These fossilized, beveled points were found by Frank Payne and described by Dr. L. S. Cressman as foreshafts. Found on the blown lake bed of Lower Klamath Lake, they are on display in the Klamath County Museum.

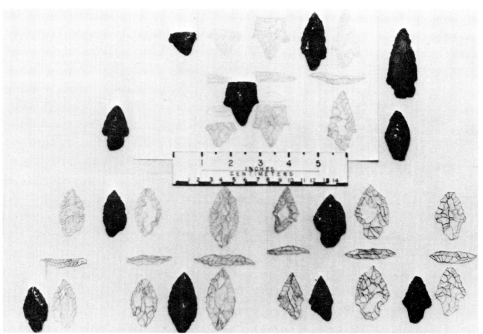

CAMEL CULTURE POINTS—Archaeologists looked in vain for the Siskiyou County camel eater's camp during the Nightfire excavation. It appears that Ray Mattson found the shoreline location of the camp. These points are quite different from later Modoc, and even older Modoc points. They resemble Pinto Basin points more than Klamath country projectiles. The site has never been excavated.

Prehistoric Indian camp sites were first revealed around the edge of the lake and on the islands. The soil then moved from the lower levels of the lake giving it the aspect of a sandy desert.

Frank Payne, an early day amateur collector, made arrangements with his employer, Merle West, to search the lake after the more violent dust storms. His carefully documented collection of artifacts was purchased by the Winema Hotel and a group of amateur collectors raised the money to buy the collection for the Klamath County Museum. My own visits to the dry lake bed started about 1933. By 1935, I had courage enough to drive farther through the sand and peat banks. Here in one of the lowest parts of the lake, I discovered a nearly completed assemblage of tools - manos, knives, a pipe, projectile points and a fossil bone pointed object. With the tools there was a group of fossil bones. Most of the materials, together with the bones, were given to Dr. L.S. Cressman, head of the Oregon Museum of Natural History at Eugene. The bones were identified as camel by Dr. Arnold Shotwell. The bone point was identified as a lance foreshaft.

Microlith

The ancient, wind-blown sands of Siskiyou County have yielded another bit of evidence, more unusual and perhaps more significant than any yet reported. It is common for me to get calls from amateur collectors as they know of my interest and like to exchange information. I was not too excited when my friend reported finding a fossilized bone point together with fossil wood. I asked permission to borrow the specimens in order to photograph them. The wood specimens appear to be calcified marsh plants. To my amazement, the fossil bone spear

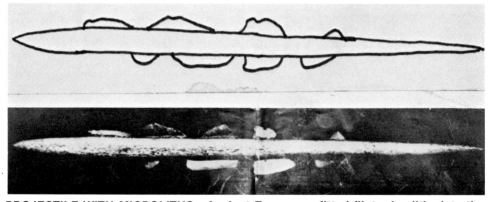

PROJECTILE WITH MICROLITHS—Ancient Europeans fitted flint microliths into the sides of this fossil bone foreshaft. A thin groove was cut with a burin, then indented into the bone to give greater killing power to the projectile point.

(Photo from Jacques Borday "First tools of Mankind" Natural History Jan. 1959)

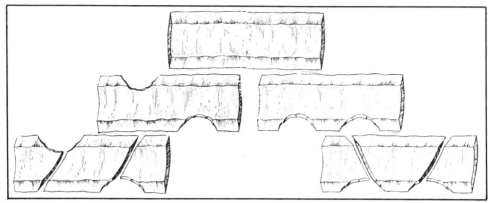

MICROLITH MANUFACTURE—In order to make microliths that could be mounted on a bone shaft, the early flint knappers of Europe struck thin spalls from a core of flint or chert. Then they broke them into small sharp pieces by the technique shown above.

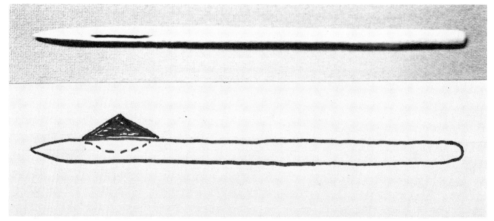

FOSSIL BONE MICROLITH SPEAR—This amazing discovery was made in Siskiyou County by Thomas Thomson of Klamath Falls. The groove for the microlith is plainly visible in the side of the bone. The drawing indicates the probable mounting for the stone chip.

ELEPHANT VERTEBRAE—Several sites on the former bed of Tule Lake have yielded elephant bones. These were uncovered by excavation for an irrigation ditch. Since there are two, it seems very likely that other bones are present. The projectile point was found nearby but there is no positive evidence that it was associated with the fossil bones.

18

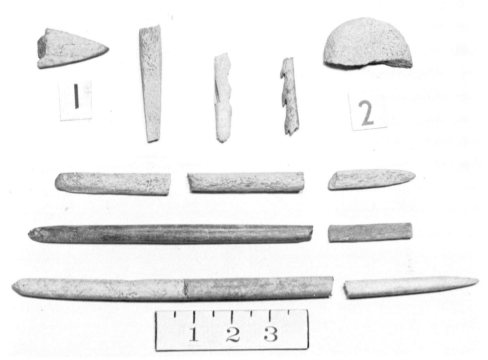

FOSSILIZED ARTIFACTS—The fossil bone javelin points found on the blown-off bed of Silver Lake resemble some found in Alaska and described in National Geographic. Some have been beveled for attachment to a shaft, a few were barbed. The object above No. 1 in the photo has been made from a large antler. No. 2 was a large fossil bone disc.

SILVER LAKE POINTS—Uncovered by wind on the Silver Lake bed, these rather unconventional points may belong with the fossil bone projectiles. Since erosion placed all objects on the same plane surface, old and recent Paiute points were sometimes found together. The two upper objects called concave base are known to be very old.

point had been grooved out with a burin in order to hold a microlith. Microliths were used by the ancient people of Europe by inserting pieces of flint or chert on the sides of their bone projectiles to give them greater cutting surface. I have never heard of such use of microliths in the western states. Since the spear is obviously fossilized and very old, and since its shape is entirely different from the foreshafts in the Payne collection, I am led to wonder if it was made by

19

different people than the camel eaters. Were they living in Siskiyou County at the same time? The periods of occupation of the Indians in all areas was so great that a couple of centuries mean little now but would be sufficient for a group to move on or even become extinct and the sites reoccupied by a different tribe.

Silver Lake Ancients

A fourth type of Paleo Indian culture has been found on the dry bed of Silver Lake in northern Lake County. Here too, the major difference from others, such as Windust or Fort Rock Cave, is indicated by the fossilized bone artifacts. These consist of: large cylindrical javelin points (unbeveled), heavy barbed points, a three inch disk made from the bone of a large mammal, a decorated paddle made from the bone of a large mammal. These objects are not like the isolated occurrence of the microlith - type spear. More than twenty such pieces were found in the dry years of 1933-38.

The big question - Why were not such objects found in the campsites and hunting places of the neighboring ancient people? Certainly conditions were present in most sites to cause fossilization of the bone tools. The chipped objects from the wind-whipped lake bed also appear to be slightly different from the Windust phase points toward the east. Such a variety of projectiles were lost by the occupants of the marshy depressions over so many centuries that distinguishing a single age group is pure guess work. One Clovis point was reported at Silver Lake, now in the Favell Museum; also a few points there resemble Windust.

Scientists, especially archaeologists, must remain skeptical until proof is offered. The nagging thought and possibility remains. Were the inhabitants discussed by Emma Lou Davis, living in the marshy basins of the Jefferson State long before any of us could dream they were?

MYSTERY OF THE CRESCENTS

The California Indian Museum near Sutter's Fort in Sacramento, California, is a tremendously interesting place. When we left, after visiting there in 1966, I was enthusiastic. I had just found confirmation of a theory on the purpose and use of the crescent-shaped, chipped, stone objects. Collectors had found them in the Klamath country east of the Cascades but had no plausible explanation for their use.

I was now satisfied that a friend's idea was correct - that the stones, mostly colored, were used by the Indian doctors called conjurers or shamen. In theory, they were part of magic along with incantations in the healing arts.

I wrote in Ancient Tribes of the Klamath Country: "He thought the crescent was hidden in the hand or mouth, then either pulled from the mouth of the shaman or from some part of the ill person's body."

Critical comments about this theory were fended off by reference to the California State Museum and by questioning the critic as to what he might suggest for their use. We even named a site "Shaman's Camp" because we found several of these rather rare stones there.

As time passed, I felt less positive about the use of these attractive stones. Friends reported finding them on bare alkali flats - a strange place for a doctor's office, even an Indian doctor.

A rock dealer in Hawthorne, Nevada, told of a California couple who found numerous crescents in northern Nevada. The literature of the time told very little about them in terms of their purpose or use. Amateur collectors of Indian artifacts called them: moon stones, worship stones, scrapers and "fish gutters."

As time progressed, more learned and sometimes reasonable theories were proposed regarding the use of these chipped artifacts. The facts simply did not support their use as shaman stones although the Indian conjurers might have used them on rare occasions. Other explanations, while plausible, lacked the evidence necessary to form a reasonable conclusion.

Since virtually all crescents were surface finds and in the possession of amateur collectors, it would take a major effort to gather valid information. With the encouragement of a couple of professional archaeologists, the board of the Great Basin Associates, an organization of amateur collectors, decided to make a study of the crescents available for measurement and record. A committee of five was selected to evaluate the information and then try to determine the purpose of the stones.

Since we had no precedent for the study, new terminology had to be developed to be sure participants in the study had a common purpose. A description of the the specimens was sent out as in Fig. 1

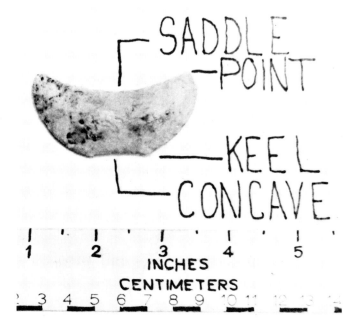

FIGURE #1—Parts of a Crescent.

showing the parts.

Requests were made to report: the color, length, depth; whether the keel or saddle was ground, if the keel was round, flat or concave; location and type of site, whether river, lake, dry lake, mound or other. They were also asked to draw an outline around the specimens and, if possible, to identify the type of rock from which the crescent was flaked. The following report form, Fig. 2 was sent in quantity to collectors who were requested to report on any that were complete enough to be sure of the information.

Color __GREY__
Length __?__ __BROKEN__
Depth __3/4 INCH__
Grinding- Absent _____
       Keel _____
      Saddle _____
      Both __X__
Location __SILVER LAKE__
Type of site __PLAYA LAKE BED__
Reported by __JOHN DOE__

Keel- Round _____
    Flat _____
    Concave __X__

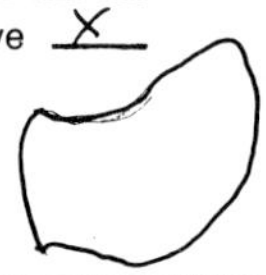

FIGURE #2—Report Form.

Reports on more than 300 crescents were received by the committee although some were received after the study had been summarized. Midway through the study, it was discovered that Dr. Lewis W. Tadlock of U.C.L.A. had made a study entitled "Certain Crescentic

Stone Objects as a Time Marker in the Western United States."
Tadlock too had studied the collections of amateurs but lacked certain information about them.

Steve Wallman, who served as a member of the G.B.A. study committee, had done extensive exploration in the Black Rock Desert of Nevada and had written a paper for the Oregon Archaeological Society publication "Screenings."

One thing that all professional and amateurs agree on is that the manufacture and use of crescents goes far back in antiquity. Dr. William Wallace in the Handbook of American Indians (California Edition) reported, "The only classes of artifacts typical of the first period of occupation comprise fluted points and chipped stone crescents."

Dr. Emma Lou Davis reported crescents of great age found at China Lake and Lake Hill Island in California, as well as in a Clovis associated tool kit at Lake Mohave. The G.B.A. study certainly confirmed the matter of antiquity. Some extensive collections made on more recent sites contained no crescents.

Dick Poole assembled the reports and compiled the statistical information. He converted measurements to sixteenth inch descriptions as follows:

	Smallest	Average	Largest
Length	12/16	1 12/16	3 inches
Depth	4/16	12/16	1 8/16

The shape of the crescent might also have a bearing on the uses intended by the maker. There was a round keel on 170 or 57.8%, 93 or 31.6% had a flat keel and 31 or 10.5% had a concave keel.

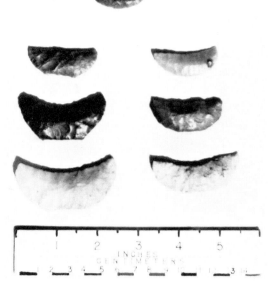

FIGURE #3—Group of typical Crescents all colored. Those on the left have been flattened or made concave on the keel as though for a point of attachment.

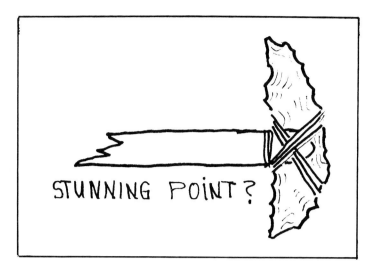

FIGURE #4—Stunning Point?

It was not uncommon for ancient or archaic Indians to grind their projectile points or articles which were prepared for attachment to a shaft or handle. This characteristic was sometimes difficult to determine but the survey showed grinding was absent on 162 or 55.6%. The keel was ground on 39 or 13.4%, the saddle on 23 or 7.9%. Both keel and saddle were ground on 67 or 23%.

Some, including Wallace, have felt that grinding was an indication that the crescents were mounted on a shaft for a projectile point as in Fig. 4. Their purpose was to stun waterfowl. Since the bow and arrow was invented only about 2700 years ago, about 10,000 years after the invention of the crescent, this use seems unlikely to the writer.

The stone material from which the crescents were made also provided a clue to their purpose. Projectile points found in the region are mostly made of obsidian, 80 to 90%. Amazingly, only 30 (of the 300) or 10.4% were made of obsidian. It is difficult for amateur collectors to identify gem rocks. Even expert rockhounds often disagree but the following table reports the type of stones as near as possible:

Agate or chert	88 - 30.5%	Obsidian	30 - 10.4%
Quartz	4 - 1.4%	Jasper	49 - 17.0%
Petrified Wood	2 - .7%	Basalt	9 - 3.1%
Unknown	106 - 36.8%		

It is natural that our numbers show a lot of unknown. Some of our research committee believe that the stones may have been selected for purposes of heat treatment in order to make them flake properly and hold an edge.

A very unusual and important bit of information gathered by G.B.A. relates to the color of the crescents. Normally black (obsidian) would be expected to predominate. Actually lighter colors were found in larger numbers as in the following table:

Clear	7 · 2.4%	Yellow	56 · 19.5%
Grey	32 · 11.2%	White	29 · 10.1%
Orange	9 · 3.1%	Blue	2 · .7%
Red	19 · 6.6%	Black	49 · 17.0%
Pink	7 · 2.4%	Green	5 · 1.7%
Brown	66 · 22.9%	Brown Moss	7 · 2.4%

The geographical location of the crescent finds were very much in agreement with the areas described by Tadlock. Since Indians were also avid collectors of artifacts there no doubt has been some redistribution even though very few were found on sites that could be considered less than 8,000 years old. Sites reported were as follows:

Location:	Northern Nevada	# 127 · 44.7%
	Malheur County	70 · 24.6
	Modoc County	39 · 13.7
	Oregon Desert**	36 · 12.7
	Klamath, Link & Lost Rivers	5 · 1.8
	Agency & Klamath Lakes	7 · 2.5

** Oregon Desert includes Lake County, Silver Lake, Christmas Valley, Fort Rock

Probably the most significant and revealing information in the study, and information that has not previously been described, related to the type of site upon which the crescents were found. The following results were tabulated by Poole:

Type of Site	Dry Lake Beds**	# 230 · 81.2%
	Existing Lake Shore	36 · 12.7
	Camp Midden	11 · 3.9
	Riverbanks	5 · 1.8
	Foothills	1 · .3

** Dry Lake Beds includes alkali flats and playa wet weather lakes.

The overwhelming evidence shows that the users of these crescentic objects lived around the lakes and marshes that once filled the flat basins in between the fault scarps of the Great Basin.

The Black Rock Desert of Nevada and similar geological structures into Oregon provided the greatest numbers of specimens. Steve Wallman reported that in the early days while hunting there sometimes five to twenty-five crescents could be found in a very limited radius. Wallman thinks that objects were used as general purpose knives in handling the animals killed by the ancient hunters.

FIGURE #5—Elephant kill site.

Both Columbian elephants and Bison Antiquus fossils have been found in the Black Rock Desert, Fig. 5. The type of colored stone he believes was selected to be heat treated in order to hold a better cut-

FIGURE #6—Crescent used as a spokeshave.

ting edge. Tools associated with the Black Rock tool kit are burins, gravers, Clovis fluted points and what Wallman calls "Black Rock Concaves," which resemble Clovis points except for the fluted sides. It is possible that the concave points could have preceded the fluted points.

A spokeshave was a tool used by the old coachmakers and wheelwrights to round out and smooth the wooden spokes of wagon wheels and carriages. Archaeologists have adapted the term to describe certain chipped stone pieces made with a curvature on one or more sides. Some scientists believe the crescents were made for smoothing and rounding the shafts of their spears and tools as in Fig. 6.

The curved shape, as well as the concave keel on many of the stones, indicates that such a use was practical. A question - Why would so many be made of colored stone and why should the manufacture of the shafts be done on playa lake beds?

Another solution to the mystery of these interesting stones could be that they were used in the fishing industry either as lures or fish hooks. The colored material would be attractive to fish. Some crescents were ground as though for attachment to a line. Even more

FIGURE #7—Giant Cutthroat trout.

(Neveda Fish and Game Commission)

FIGURE #8—Crescent used as a fish lure.

(Courtesy Ron Poole)

convincing is the location on the shores or beds of the former pluvial lakes of the Great Basin.

Question: Wouldn't the stones be far too large for use as fish hooks? At Walker Lake near Hawthorne, Nevada, and Pyramid Lake in northern Nevada, we have the remains of lakes that were once a part of a great series of post-pliestocene water bodies. These have been described by Sessions Wheeler as Lake Lahontan. In both of these lakes can be found giant trout, some as large as 64 pounds. Fremont called the fish "salmon trout" and succeeded in keeping his exploring party alive by trading for the fish from the Indians. Fig. 7 shows a picture taken by the Nevada Fish and Game Commission. It is obviously big enough to swallow even the largest of the stone crescents. Fig. 8 by artist Ron Poole illustrates their use as a fish lure.

FIGURE #9—Ice Breaker.

(Courtesy Favell Museum)

Additional clues to use in solving the mystery of the crescents should be consideration of the tools in association with the location and age. Research by L. L. Loud of the University of California at Lovelock Cave revealed stone tools called ice breakers. Fig. 9 shows three from Nevada now in the Favell Museum in Klamath Falls. So far as I can determine, such ice breakers have been found only in the same geographical areas as crescents. Fig. 10 was found near the flat basin of Summer Lake by J. Paul Matthews.

What ever happened to Shaman's Camp? It is now blown-off and

FIGURE #10—
Summer Lake Ice
Breaker.

barren. We also now know it was misnamed - even I can be wrong once! Shaman's Camp was located on a slightly sloping edge of a large post-glacial lake. Steven Bedwell said the lake once covered the entire Fort Rock and Christmas Valley. The ancient occupants fished and hunted waterfowl in the lake. They also probably hunted the elephants, camels, sloths and other large mammals whose fossil bones have been uncovered by desert winds in nearby Fossil Lake.

The archaic occupants left behind, in addition to several crescents, numerous chips of colored rock that had been carried some distance and an obsidian spear or dart point about four inches long. It was without shoulders and had a flat base. Several strange chipped stone objects of agate were found that we called "slugs." They are now believed to be blanks to be worked into crescentic shape or rejects from stone knapping efforts. A beautiful pink chert spear point was also found but it has a stem and does not seem to belong to the same age as other objects found in the camp.

Is the mystery of the crescents solved? The members of the Great Basin Associates committee could not agree. As great as democracy may be, we cannot vote ourselves into a valid scientific conclusion. The study, however, provided new and valuable information. - Information that was obtainable only from a large number of people who had hunted and kept the results of their walks of hundreds of miles over many years.

THE MYSTERY OF PETROGLYPH POINT

The mountain does not look like the typical cone shaped volcano. It appears rather flat on top as the former crater has more of a saucer-like indentation. It can be seen across the flat bed of the Tule Lake Basin for ten or fifteen miles and looks as though a giant knife had cut off one side leaving a steep vertical cliff.

There are two reasons the former volcano looks different. Geologists say the eruption took place underwater where the ash, pumice and cinders were fused by intense heat into a compact sandstone-like material called palogonite tuff. The second reason the mountain looks different is because of its location at the end of a peninsula extending into Tule Lake. Over the hundreds of centuries since the original eruption, the waves and ice, driven by the strong winds from the west, have cut away one side of the mountain.

The height of the steep cliff-face rises about 170 feet above the floor of the basin. The brown tuff has had repeated periods of flooding until the waters have deposited calcium and minerals making it white in the lower portions. This formed an ideal surface for the designs of the primitive artists.

The calcified face of the extinct volcano shows the height of previous water levels. The wineglass-shaped carving (upper center) was often referred to by early writers, sometimes as a Phonecian ship or other exciting reproduction.

Photo by Hal Ogle

The incised figures and designs extend for over a quarter mile along an undercut carved by the wave action at the base of the mountain. Most are from 6 to 9 feet above ground level but some are more than 25 feet high. It is apparent that it was necessary for the ancient rock artists to work from a raft or boat in order to reach the level of the carvings. It is also apparent that the water level of Tule Lake has varied substantially over the period of centuries.

Aside from Crater Lake and Mount Shasta, no geological natural feature has inspired more journalistic efforts than this strange cliff now called Petroglyph Point. In terms of pure imagination, nothing can match the exciting offerings of the various writers. Helen Crotty, in a research project for U.C.L.A., surveyed some of the early literature describing the rock art:

"The earliest known published reference to Petroglyph Point appeared in the **Sacramento Bee** October 11, 1923. The story (anonymous 1923) credits J.D. Howard with "disproving" the theory of other observers that the carvings could have been made by Indians. Indians, according to Howard, made "pictures" by scratching on soft sandstone, but the people who had inscribed the Tule Lake writings had "characters" like those of the Egyptians or Phoenicians, and they had cut the letters deeply into the "hard" rock.

"Brown accepted the carvings as the work of Indians, but not the Modocs. His first account ascribes the "hieroglyphics" to a little-known tribe of "Rock Indians" who, centuries earlier, had been "exterminated down to the last individual" by the fierce Modocs, "one of the most warlike and cruel tribes in the whole west." The second article, while dwelling on the Modoc reputation for raiding neighboring tribes for slaves and for massacring white immigrants and settlers, omits any reference to "Rock Indians" but relates a "vague tradition" among the Modocs about a race who vanished from the Tule Lake region "in the wake of a white-haired goddess who enticed them to their doom" along a subterranean river through the Lava beds. Brown reports a design that he sees as "a perfect reproduction of a boat-shaped lamp such as was in use in eastern countries about the time of the beginning of the Christian era."

The most extravagant claims about the petroglyphs, however, appeared in the Portland Oregonian in November 1929 under the by-line of John W. Kelly. The author is confident that "No Indian would carve a cliff for a quarter-mile. In no respect do these carvings resemble the familiar Indian paintings so common in all parts of the Oregon country." Instead, the reader is assured that "Klamath basin was peopled with considerable number of men and women who had a written language before the Genovese navigator sailed in the Santa Maria. They were in Klamath country possibly 1,000 years ago." The writing is identified as of two systems: one suggesting the "ogam [sic] writing of the Druids of ancient Ireland, England, Scotland, and Wales," while the second system "is on the order of the runes of the Scandinavian countries." Some of the latter, it is claimed, had been " identified as Runic and Gothic and translated as such within the past few days." As for the Ogham, it is described as a sort of shorthand, in which perpendicular or diagonal lines cross a long horizontal one, with meaning dependent on the number of strokes and their position above or below the line. Kelly explains that J.D. Howard, in painting the carvings to make them more visible in photographs, had failed to recognize the importance of minor dots and dashes, and therefore the Ogham and most of the Runes, could not be translated. The "perfectly formed" lamp, however, has now become the "sacred lamp of the Druids" and is reported to occur at least twice, among the "many repetitions" of the "sacred oak of the Druids (Kelly 1929).

Kelly's story was apparently elaborated into a news service feature article the following year (Anonymous 1930). The author proposes that the carvings were made by Irish pioneers who lived in America 1000 years ago. He claims that historians find it credible that a tribe of hardy, adventurous Milesian Celts might have penetrated the Bering Straits and reached North America while their kinsmen migrated westward from Egypt through Spain to settle in Ireland. Failing this, they might have crossed the Pacific, or some "long-forgotten Irish sailors" might have made it across the Atlantic and then wandered to the wilds of Oregon long before Columbus discovered America. No hypothesis, it seems is too preposterous to explain how these carvings "almost identical in character with famous Druid stone writings found in Ireland" could have appeared at Tule Lake."

I have seen charts prepared by an amateur journalist archaeologist with hours of tedious work seeking to prove that the "writings" were Runic. Most writers made reference to J. D. Howard as a source of information. I knew Howard only slightly but he had the reputation of being an excellent scientist in the field of botany and geology. A friend, who knew him well, said that he had a strange and active sense of humor and he may have been purposely leading the reporters along false paths which they eagerly followed. I think it more likely that Howard, who carried on a long one-man crusade to have the region made into a national monument, used the stories to attract national attention to the area.

It is fortunate that Helen Crotty had the interest and determination to make an extensive and scholarly study of Petroglyph Point. Countless hours of photographing, measuring and examining the figures was later followed by comparing them with the petroglyphs in other regions. Her work which started back in 1959 was assisted by

SYMBOL BRIDGE PAINT-INGS—Called pictographs, the paintings at Symbol Bridge in the Modoc Lava Beds have mostly different designs from those at Petroglyph Point. The one that appears at upper left is found at both sites. I have called it water bug."

Photo taken by Judson Howard more than 70 years ago.

national park personnel. The report titled **Petroglyph Point Revisited: A Modoc County Site** has been published as a part of U.C.L.A. monograph XX "Messages From The Past" under the direction of Dr. Clement W. Weighan.

Mrs. Crotty has performed a valuable service in stripping away the false information about Petroglyph Point. In addition, she has solved a part of the mystery by determining who made the inscriptions. She carefully copied the designs and grouped them into four classifications as follows: Possible Representational, Curvilinear Abstract, Reclilinear Abstract and Mixed. It is significant that only 1.5% appear to represent actual humanoids or objects.

It was much easier for the Indian artist to work on the soft tuff surface of Petroglyph Point than on harder basalt rocks of the region. This may in some measure account for the great number and variety of forms. It also permitted the technique of rubbing and scraping rather than the pecking and pounding required on harder surfaces.

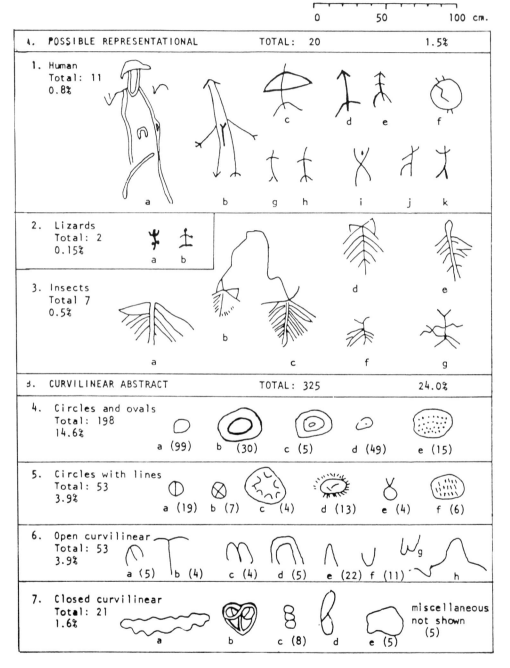

TOTAL NUMBER OF ELEMENTS 1358

APPROXIMATE SCALE: 1:20

0   50   100 cm.

1. POSSIBLE REPRESENTATIONAL   TOTAL: 20   1.5%

1. Human
Total: 11
0.8%

a   b   c   d   e   f   g   h   i   j   k

2. Lizards
Total: 2
0.15%

a   b

3. Insects
Total 7
0.5%

a   b   c   d   e   f   g

3. CURVILINEAR ABSTRACT   TOTAL: 325   24.0%

4. Circles and ovals
Total: 198
14.6%

a (99)   b (30)   c (5)   d (49)   e (15)

5. Circles with lines
Total: 53
3.9%

a (19)   b (7)   c (4)   d (13)   e (4)   f (6)

6. Open curvilinear
Total: 53
3.9%

a (5)   b (4)   c (4)   d (5)   e (22)   f (11)   g   h

7. Closed curvilinear
Total: 21
1.6%

a   b   c (8)   d   e (5)   miscellaneous not shown (5)

Many of the markings are simple straight vertical lines, sometimes placed in groups. There are also great numbers of simple dots made by poking a hole in the white calcified surface with a sharp instrument.

34

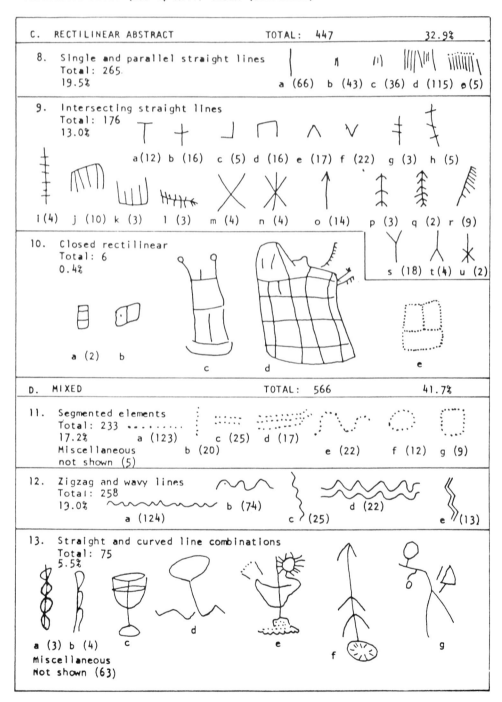

C. RECTILINEAR ABSTRACT   TOTAL: 447   32.9%

8. Single and parallel straight lines
    Total: 265.
    19.5%
                                    a (66) b (43) c (36) d (115) e (5)

9. Intersecting straight lines
    Total: 176
    13.0%
                a(12) b (16) c (5) d (16) e (17) f (22) g (3) h (5)

    i(4) j (10) k (3) l (3) m (4) n (4) o (14) p (3) q (2) r (9)

    s (18) t (4) u (2)

10. Closed rectilinear
    Total: 6
    0.4%

    a (2) b   c   d   e

D. MIXED   TOTAL: 566   41.7%

11. Segmented elements
    Total: 233
    17.2%   a (123)
    Miscellaneous   b (20)   c (25)   d (17)
    not shown (5)   e (22)   f (12)   g (9)

12. Zigzag and wavy lines
    Total: 258
    13.0%   b (74)   d (22)
              a (124)   c (25)   e (13)

13. Straight and curved line combinations
    Total: 75
    5.5%

                                    d
    a (3) b (4)   c   e   f   g
    Miscellaneous
    Not shown (63)

Some archaeologists have placed the date 3,000 years before present as the earliest date for the petroglyphs. I think some of them are much older. The Modocs did not live in great population groups. The very numbers and extent of the designs would indicate a long

35

time period for their execution. Indians living in the vicinity indicated no knowledge of these petroglyphs when white settlers entered the basin.

Further, the studies at Nightfire Island proved a long period of occupation of over 7,000 years by the Modocs. Some artifacts found near the Point were obviously made before the invention of the bow and arrow about 2700 years ago. A final bit of evidence- many of the pictograph (painted) designs at other Modoc sites are different from those on Petroglyph Point.

The study by Mrs. Crotty and that of other scientists have taken away the mystery about who made the stone inscriptions. But the mystery of why they were made remains. It would take substantial motivation to cause a Modoc to go by canoe or raft to the face of the volcanic cliff, then stand up in the treacherous craft to incise the designs. Some Indian rock art depicts game animals and were thought to bring luck in hunting or fishing. This type is absent at Tule Lake. Another explanation offered was that the inscriptions were made in the quest for spirit power. While this is reasonable, why not make the inscriptions in a more accessible place?

My theory for the second part of the mystery has its origin in the Modoc legend that was related to Jeremiah Curtin in 1884 by a Modoc Indian woman, Koalakaka. It told of the Modoc man who had bad luck gambling and had lost all of his property. His mother told him to go and visit the owl rock. After this his luck improved. Petroglyph Point is the father of all owl rocks. The wind and the weather has eroded hundreds of cavities and benches in the upper part of the cliff's face. Many owls carrying rodents and mice fly there to digest their food, make nests and feed their offspring.

The thousands of fur-ball pellets dropped behind the protective fence attest the number of owls and their capability of catching rodents.

In the Modoc culture, the owls had a special place. Their hoot was significant and their power was respected. Could the hundreds of generations of owls have been the attraction that made the Modoc gamblers visit there to pray for spirit power and luck? The vast number of dots and vertical lines suggest a calendar or scoreboard. I think Petroglyph Point in the Modoc Lava Beds National Monument is the Owl Rock of Modoc legend- a place to pray and seek power.

OWL NEST CREVICES—Winds have cut crevices in the softer layers of the volcanic tuff. These provide owls with ideal perches on which to nest and digest the furry rodents caught on the shores of Tule Lake.

OWL PELLETS—Owls have no gizzard so eject the indigestible material in the form of furry, oval-shaped balls. By examining the contents of the pellets their food habits can be determined. Thousands of such pellets are dropped each year from the face of "Owl Rock" (Petroglyph Point). Most girls do not like to examine the furry shaped balls but Susie Atiyeh, daughter of Governor Atiyeh, finds them quite interesting.

MODOC FISH TRAP

A windy stormy day is often referred to as "good weather for ducks." Actually, I believe such a day is good weather for duck hunters but bad weather for ducks.

Ducks and geese fly a lot more on stormy days because of their discomfort on the ponds and rivers and because it is harder to feed in the wind. Under such conditions, they often group up and stand on the shore.

This day was bad weather for hunters-clear, cold and sunny. The hunters gave up and left Lost River early. As their boat came down the river a semi-submerged object was observed in the river which attracted their attention. Finally they became curious and turned the boat back to have a closer look. It was almost covered by water plants but a network of woven willows could be seen intertwined with the green weeds.

When a knock came on my door, I was still drinking Sunday morning coffee. The hunter said, "I have something to show you." Expecting to see ducks or geese, I walked to the back of his pickup. I was amazed and thrilled at what I saw- a woven willow fish trap.

For several years I had tried to locate a picture of a Modoc or Klamath fish trap. Neither museums, Indians or basket collectors

MODOC FISH TRAP—The large end of the cone-shaped trap is about 18 inches wide. The funnel leading into the trap has an opening of about 8 inches.

38

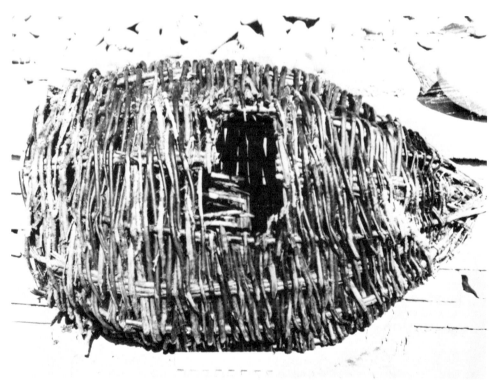

TRAP DOOR—An opening at the side enabled fish to be dumped when the trap was picked up. A point of attachment was made at the small end so the entrance faced downstream.

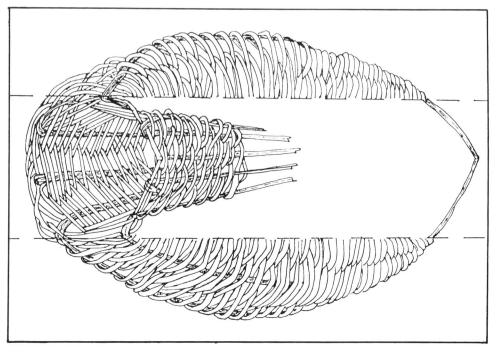

WILLOW CONSTRUCTION—Artist Nora Rock's drawing shows how skillfully the Modoc weavers made the trap so the chubs could get in to where the bait was kept but could not get out.

TUI CHUBS—These fish netted by Dr. Richard Wilson for the Nightfire Island research project were a popular and plentiful Modoc food. The fish reach a length of about 12 inches and are quite nutritious.

could locate one. The Smithsonian supplied a picture of a Klamath fish net but denied possessing a Modoc fish trap or a picture of one.

Since wooden objects or bone objects, which have been preserved by being imbedded in mud, quickly deteriorate when removed from the water I advised the owner to remove the water plants and wash off the mud. Then as soon as the surface dried, to chemically treat it each time it appeared to be dry enough. It is now preserved in excellent condition.

The cone-shaped trap was woven to be attached with the small end of the cone upstream. It is too small to serve in catching mullet and, since Lost River was never a good trout stream, it is assumed that its principal use was for tui chubs.

A cleverly made door was designed to open toward the inside. After much study, it was reassembled to show how it functioned.

It seems remarkable that an object made of wood could survive. The fact is that mud seems to be an excellent preservative. At the Ozette archaeological site in Washington, an entire village buried in mud is being excavated. Hundreds of wooden objects have been preserved in this airless stratum.

When the Upper Klamath Lake is low, it is not unusual that wooden objects such as canoe paddles or bows are washed out and found rather well preserved. If they are not recovered and treated with preservatives, they soon (within hours) will curl up and disintegrate.

Thanks to an alert and interested duck hunter, this rare object showing the basketry skill and fishing habits of the Lost River Modocs has been preserved.

BEN WRIGHT
ANGEL OR DEVIL

If a poll were taken among the Modoc Indians to decide who they believed to be the most evil man in history, the choice would over-whelming go to Ben Wright. An opinion survey among the descendants of early immigrants into Siskiyou and Jackson County would bring about a very different result. Writers of history too disagree on the qualities of this strange man.

Don Fisher, a former history teacher, who was later superintendent of the Lava Beds National Monument, did extensive research on Wright. His work was given to me by courtesy of the Siskiyou County Historical Society. Fisher wrote:

"I will devote the rest of my life seeking revenge for her death." Thus spoke a seventeen year old boy as he gazed at the still form of his sweetheart of a few weeks, the victim of an attack by Indians on an immigrant trail in 1847.

"The young man who made the vow was Benjamin Wright, later to gain fame and notoriety as an Indian fighter, and perhaps the man who was the principal cause of the Modoc War; the only Indian war of any importance that occured in California."

Wright's 1847 party reached the Oregon Country shortly after the massacre of Dr. Marcus Whitman's people. He immediately enlisted as a volunteer and established an enviable reputation for bravery and skill.

Don Fisher reports,"Following this campaign, Wright became a hunter and trapper. He finally settled at Cottonwood, California, about twenty miles from the present town of Yreka, California. From here he roamed over the country, far and wide, hunting, trapping or shooting Indians; living in fact, like the Indians themselves. Dressed in buckskin, his glossy black hair reached his waist. It is said that he took

BEN WRIGHT—Early fron-tiersmen did not wear long hair so much for appearance but rather as a "macho" sign of bravery. A good scalp made a person a more likely target and offered a challenge to the opponents.

Courtesy Siskiyou Co. Museum

pride in acting like an Indian and in his dealings with them, scalping the dead, and committing other barbarities, such as cutting off the ears, nose and fingers of the wounded. He fought Indians because of his vow and because of his love for excitement.

"Wright was very proud of his long hair and refused to have it cut; although his men begged him to do so. Later it almost cost him his life. While encamped on Willow Creek, the Modocs attempted to stampede the horses. Wright was the first to rush toward the picket line and in the darkness, one of his men, mistaking Wright for an In-dian, seized him by the hair and was preparing to plunge a knife into him, thinking him a Modoc, when the mistake was discovered.

"In the summer of 1851, the Modocs were very active in stealing livestock from ranchers living in Shasta Valley. In a raid near Butteville they took forty-six mules and horses; twenty-five of which belonged to the packtrain of Augustus Meamber. After this raid, the settlers became desperate and decided to organize a volunteer company to pursue the Indians and recover the stock. It was decided to send for Ben Wright. He arrived accompanied by two friendly Indians but refus-ed the position of captain, preferring to fight in the ranks.

"William R. Fanning, who was a member of the party, gave the following partial list of the members: Samuel Smith, Captain, Ben Wright, guide and scout, George Rodgers, Morris Rodgers, Henry Smith, William Brown, William Kershaw, Lin Able, Frank Tomlinson, Frank Fawset, Jacob Rhoads, John Onsley, August Meamber, two Spaniards, one called Dobe John, and two Oregon Indians, Swill and Enos.

"Plans were then made for the expedition. Each member of the company was equipped with a rifle, pistol, and a supply of ammunition. N. D. Julian furnished a quantity of beef. When everything was in readiness the party started for the Modoc country.

"The route from Yreka to the Modoc country was east to Sheep Rock thence to Grass Lake then east to a point called Hole in the Ground, near the present town of Dorris, California, then eastward around lower Klamath Lake then north to the ford on Willow Creek, to the Natural Bridge on Lost River, near the present town of Merrill, Oregon, around the shore of Tule Lake to a point a few miles south of the present town of Malin, Oregon, then east to Clear Lake, a distance of approximately one hundred fifteen miles."

It was near the natural bridge where a Modoc village was located. Here considerable livestock was held by the Indians. The men were eager to attack immediately but were persuaded by Wright to wait. Pretending to appear as an immigrant party. they quietly approached the camp. Next morning at dawn a surprise attack was made. A part of the horses and cattle was recovered. As the supplies were getting low, the cattle were killed and the meat dried.

Following this battle, Wright finally induced the Indians to meet under a flag of truce. The Modocs agreed to return the livestock and refrain from further raids. The Wright party in turn agreed to return to Yreka. The Indians then returned some horses and cattle.

Wright and his party started for Yreka but at their first camp on Willow Creek the Indians attacked and captured eleven horses. This made the whites decide to continue their war. Four men were dispatched to Yreka for supplies as the weather was cold and food was low.

When the supplies arrived, an attack was made on an island village at the mouth of Lost River. Several of Wright's men were wounded with arrows but twenty-seven women and children and three men were captured. They all expected to be killed but when this did not occur, they agreed to talk. After being offered freedom in exchange for serving as guides, they led the Yreka party to the Indian Village. The inhabitants took refuge in a well-protected cave. After futilely trying to attack the cave, the volunteers decided to try to smoke them out. Fires were burned at the cave entrance for twenty-four hours without effect on the stubborn Modocs. The attempt was

MODOC HABITAT—The rough volcanic area, now the Modoc Lava Beds National Monument, provided an excellent place for the Indians to live. Caves, fortifications and impassable lava flows gave them a natural advantage in dealing with the Whites.

(Herald-News photo)

finally abandoned and the party returned to Yreka with the captured horses.

A person who has grown up and matured in a European culture will never be able to understand the reasoning or ethics of a primitive culture such as the Modocs. They did not have the restraints of a Christian background. Described as pragmatists, the Modoc philosophy was "Might is right." Their existence had depended upon their ability to take from nature, or their neighbors, whichever was more practical.

Raiding was a highly admired activity. A people, who had attacked villages and captured slaves from the Shastas, Pit Rivers and Paiutes for centuries, would not feel inhibited in attacking a wagon load of white immigrants, where the rewards were so much greater, and especially when getting them was a path to prestige. To compound the problem for immigrants and soldiers, the Modocs were exceptionally brave and aggressive. They were simply tough guys- tough

44

with each other and tough with their enemies. They were said to continue fighting when they knew the odds were against them.

In a book given to me by Bill Fallis, chairman of the Modoc Tribe of the Oklahoma Modocs, a somewhat different version has been presented by author, Odie B. Faulk. He said the Modocs did not want wagon trains passing through their summer hunting grounds. In addition, they felt the whites brought disease. The valuable horse which would provide the warrior's mobility was, of course, further incentive for immigrant raids.

By 1852 increasing numbers of wagon trains were headed for Oregon and the goldfields of California. Bloody Point on the east side of Tule Lake had become the favored point of attack for the Modocs. One man named Coffin was the sole survivor of such an attack and rode into Yreka with the story. When the citizens of Yreka learned what had occurred, they sent for Ben Wright and a company was quickly organized and equipped with arms, horses and provisions.

On September 6, a wagon train besieged by the Modocs saw another band of horsemen approaching. They feared that it was Indians coming to join in the attack. Then they saw that the horsemen had each tied a white handkerchief around his rifle. Seeing the reinforcement Fisher said,"The Indians took refuge in the tules near the lake trying to reach their canoes but the whites using rifles, pistols and knives took a terrible revenge. The scene of the fight covered a mile along the shore.

"For several days, Wright and his men searched for the victims of the Indians. Twenty-two bodies were found and buried, two of them women and one a child. All were horribly mutilated and scalped.

"Captain John E. Ross with a company of twenty-two volunteers from Jacksonville, Oregon, arrived a few days later and joined in the search. They found fourteen additional bodies, several being women and children. It was evident that several wagon trains had been captured and all of the immigrants killed.

"Wright and his men then escorted the large wagon train that had assembled at Clear Lake through the Modoc Country and then returned to their camp at Clear Lake. Here several small trains were united into a large one and then safely escorted to safety. Thus all summer and fall, Wright and his men were busy. Late in October the last train arrived and was escorted through the Modoc territory. By this time the company had been reduced to eighteen men. Captain McDermit had returned to Yreka with Judge Irwin's train.

"Wright and the seventeen men decided to remain and punish the Modocs and to try and compel the Indians to make a treaty that would insure safety to the immigrants. They also wished to recover the valuables the Indians had taken from the immigrant trains."

TULE LAKE BASIN—If emigrants were to come down the Applegate Trail today, they would see a lakebed crossed by highways and powerlines, homesteader's houses and villages where angry waves once washed the shores.

As the supply of food and ammunition was getting low, four men were sent to Yreka for additional supplies.

Mary, a Modoc woman, was sent to the Modocs with a message suggesting a peace talk. Another attempt was made the next day and when she returned, two young Indians came with her. These were feasted and sent back to their camp. The next day forty Modocs came. This continued for several days.

The camp was then moved to the Lost River, near the Natural Bridge to be closer to the expected supplies. The men were nearly starved before the supplies finally arrived. The four men had stayed to vote and also to get gloriously drunk, requiring several days to sober up and get started.

With the arrival of the supplies it is stated that Wright began to plan the extermination of the Modocs. Some writers claim that he intended to secure as much of the plunder as possible and then pick a quarrel and kill the Indians. Other writers claim that Wright had a quantity of poison and intended exterminating them in this manner. J. H. Hill, a member of the party stated that Wright intended to poison the Indians, he was not interested in peace.

Invitations were again sent out and in response about fifty Modocs came under a flag of truce and pitched their camp near Wrights. Then two camps were on the west side of Lost River about one-fourth mile above the Natural Bridge, not far from the present town of Merrill, Oregon. A beef was butchered and a feast prepared, but the Indians refused to eat. It is said that there was an Indian with the Modoc band who had lived several years among the whites and recognized poison, and told the Modocs not to eat the meat.

One night old Mary told Wright that the Modocs were planning to massacre the Whites and pleaded with him to take his men and leave. Wright immediately decided to attack the Indians. That night six men were sent across the Natural Bridge and took a position opposite the camp. The rest of them were stationed back of the camp with the Indians between them and the river. Wright went into camp and again offered the Indians the meat. They again refused to accept it. He noticed the Indians were preparing their bows. Old Mary came and sat down by the side of Wright and pointed to a young Indian and told Ben that he was his brother-in-law, the sister having been given to Wright a few days previous. Wright pulled his pistol from his holster and killed the young Indian. Wright then dropped to the ground and escaped from the camp, while the rest of the company fired over his head.

In the battle that ensued, the arrows and knives could not compete with guns. All except two of the Modocs were killed. Three of Wright's men were wounded. Litters were prepared and they started to return to Yreka. A volunteer rescue party met Wright at Sheep Rock.

Wright and his fifteen men reached town, escorted by the other company. The men were dirty, shaggy and brown from their long campaign. Indian scalps dangled from their rifles, hats, and heads of their horses. These all bore mute testimony to their successful campaign. As the party rode along the street, the enthusiasm of the crowd knew no bounds, cheers and wild yells filled the air. When the procession reached the livery stable of Burgess Brothers, the Indian slayers were lifted from their horses and carried to the saloons. Whiskey was free. That night a banquet was tendered them at the Yreka House. For weeks one grand carousel was carried on by a majority of Wright's company; although a few severed connections with the company as soon as they reached town. However, aided by the riff-raff of the town, the warriors took the town by storm. They showed their trophies, flourished their weapons and related their adventures. For awhile no one dared oppose them. Gradually the sober citizens were able to coax their fire arms away to be displayed over the various bars. Gradually the better class of citizens began to exert their influence and soon the carousel ended.

Another writer, who gave a quite different version of Ben Wright's activities, was William S. Brown in his book **California Northeast, "The Bloody Ground."** Brown, a retired forest service supervisor, wrote:

"Many conflicting stories are told of this event, a good many of which depict Wright as a coldblooded murderer. One version of the affair states that Wright invited a large number of Indians to a big feast and fed them, old and young, male and female, beef poisoned with strychnine. Another story said that he surprised a large Indian camp

47

and shot down men, women and children without mercy. The latter being the common Indian version of the affair.

"To begin with, Ben Wright was hardly the type of man who would be guilty of coldblooded calculating murders described to him. After this bloody event connected to his name, he was Indian Commissioner for the State of Oregon and at various times filled important public posts in places of trust. Known as a good Indian fighter, he was also credited in Oregon history with being fair-minded and just. He was considered one of the frontier scouts of his time. It did not exactly suit the Indians to have a man the type of Ben Wright patrolling their territory at the head of a large body of fighting frontiersmen and their losses in occasional brushes with these men prompted them to make overtures of peace. A messenger was sent to Wright proposing a meeting to draw up a peace treaty.

"Wright moved his men to the Natural Bridge on Lost River just north of Tule Lake. The Modocs locating their camp nearby. Three days were spent in feasting and several powwows were held but no sign of the white girl captives was evident. Indians and whites alike were gauging each other's strength and the watchful whitemen noticed that since its establishment, the population of the Indian camp had more than doubled with new arrivals constantly drifting in.

"The actions and demeanor of the savages satisfied Wright that some kind of treachery was intended. He determined to make the first move. Before daylight on the fourth day, the white leader quietly disposed his men around the Indian camp informing them that he would enter the camp alone. The morning being cool, Wright wore a blanket with his head passing through a hole in the middle, that being the fashion of the time. Beneath the blanket, he had a loaded pistol in each hand. Walking directly to the middle of the camp, the white leader demanded of the chief that he formerly interviewed to make good his promise to deliver the two white girl captives in the hands of the whitemen immediately. The chief made an insolent reply and told Wright that he never intended to keep his promise and that there were no white girls there but there were sufficient assembled now to kill all the whitemen in the neighboring camp. Without further parlay, Wright shot the chief dead in his tracks and ran in a zigzag manner to the Indian camp firing as he went and giving and uttering warwhoops in true Indian manner. At the sound of Wright's first shot, his followers poured a fuselage of shots into the camp killing their chief and the volleys following taking the Indians by surprise. They bravely rallied and forming a line sent a shower of arrows toward the white attackers. Wright, taking advantage gained his surprise attack, led his men in a dashing charge on the camp. It was much like an attack on an immigrant train with the opposing forces in reverse. The Indians broke

48

MODOC ROCK CIRCLES—A ranger in the Modoc Lava Beds National Monument walks through the rock rings built for habitation by the Modocs.

and fled, some hiding in the sagebrush and others jumping in the river. "Frontiersman Jenner pointed out that the Wright party returned to Yreka on November 25, 1852, penniless and almost naked and that each man knew from the start that in return for risking his life there would be no financial remuneration. His report concluded: We were without food and clothing, without money and facing a hard winter, with flour at $2. a pound."

Following his second campaign against the Modocs, Wright was appointed Indian Agent for the tribes living near the mouth of the Rogue River, the Coquilles.

In January 1856, Wright moved his office to a place called Whaleshead, at the mouth of the Rogue River, in order to keep a better check on the Indians in the region. They were becoming very restless and rumors had reached him that the Indians were planning an uprising.

Learning that attempts were being made to the Coquilles to join the hostile tribes, Wright hastened to their villages furthest from Whaleshead. Here he found members of the hostile tribes. Wright threatened to arrest these emissaries unless they left the Coquilles alone. This they promised to do and left the camps. The people living near the mouth of the Rogue River were becoming alarmed by rumors of trouble of an impending outbreak. Wright returned to the Indian village and found everything seemingly quiet and received promises of friendship from the Coquilles. These Indians were in mortal fear of an attack by the settlers because there was a large camp of hostile Indians not far away. Wright promised to have an agent appointed to protect them until the excitement abated.

Returning to the coast, Wright met an armed party of Whites enroute to the Indian Village planning on destroying it. He reported the Coquilles as being friendly and returned with the party to the Indian camp to prove his statement. He succeeded in convincing the party and also appointed one of the men as sub-agent. Wright then returned to the coast with the remainder of the party.

That Wright was acting in good faith is borne out by a letter from Collector Dunbar of Port Orford to Joel Palmer to the effect that Wright could maintain peace in his district. The letter goes on as follows: "Ben is on the jump day and night. I never saw a more energetic agent of the public. His plans are all good, there can be no doubt of it."

To learn of their plans, Wright employed an Indian named Enos, who had served with him on the expedition after the Modocs and said to be the only Indian Wright ever trusted. This Indian and his wife were ordered to mingle with the other Indians and bring reports to Wright of all they heard and saw. Time after time these two brought reports that there seemed to be no plotting against the Whites or no plans for an uprising. As a matter of fact, Enos and his wife were actually aiding the plotters. Learning that a majority of the White residents of Whaleshead would be at Big Flat, five miles up the river, on the night of February 22, at a dance, the Indians decided to strike.

Author's note: Without any strong evidence, I would suggest that the emissaries from hostile tribes that Wright tried to eject may have been missionaries for the Ghost Dance cult. This religion originated with the Paviotso Indians of western Nevada. Their belief was that by their dancing and chants, the dead Indians would be brought back, then joined by the animals to drive the white man from their land.

It was at a dance, where the decision was made that Enos, a possible convert?, would kill Wright. The Ghost Dance did not reach the Klamaths until about 1870 when authorities had a hard time stamping out the practice.

That evening while Wright was alone in his cabin, a knock was heard and in his response to his inquiry who it was, Enos informed Wright that there was an old friend there to see him. As Wright stepped out of the doorway to greet the supposed friend, Enos struck him on the head with an axe, killing him. In the attack on the agency that followed, thirty-one persons were killed.

An article written by Marie Schlotfeldt for the Herald-News February 25, 1966 gives further information on the final days of Ben

Wright. Her information is based upon letters written at Port Orford in 1856 by P. C. O'Regan:

"Enos escaped and continued to cause trouble for some time but eventually was caught and hanged. Chetcoe Jennie disappeared from the area and was not heard from again. But first she caused Wright's heart to be cut from his body and she ate part of it in retaliation for his having whipped her through the streets of Port Orford.

"Even after death, Wright continued to cause trouble for the Indians. The waist-length curly hair of which he was so proud was taken after death as was the custom. Later when the Indians were confined to the Siletz Reservation, they held stealthy dances around the grisly object.

"Eventually, Indian Agent R. B. Metcalfe learned of the ritual. Fearing another outbreak, he demanded that the scalp be given up. When his demands were met with refusal, he ordered his men to seize two Indians and hold them in custody.

"Calmly he issued his ultimatum-if the scalp was not in his hands within fifteen minutes, the two Indians would be killed. The scalp was delivered within the allotted time and so, from the face of the earth, disappeared the last mortal vestige of Ben Wright-Indian fighter."

Angel or Devil? It may be that Ben Wright did not poison the Modocs-probably because they refused the food. I doubt that he bought the strychnine to poison squirrels. It is also true that he seemed to enjoy fighting Indians.

A Devil? Probably, but if I had seen him coming as my wagon was going from the Clear Lake hills down toward Tule Lake at Bloody Point, he would have looked like an angel.

FREIGHT TEAMS AT SILVER LAKE—The enormous wool clip was taken to rail centers at Shaniko or in Nevada, then shipped east to the textile industry in New England.

(Jim Reeder collection)

LIFE IN A SHEEP CAMP

The message was out in Ireland in the early 1900's-"Don't stop in the United States, go on to Lakeview." This word was accepted and followed by Dan Murphy of County Cork in 1906. The young Irishman had relatives in New York but he did not stop there. Traveling by railroad to Reno, he then took the stage to Lakeview, Oregon.

He felt lucky that a job was offered there stacking hay near Plush. A unique problem then changed the course of his life- rattlesnakes! For a man who had never seen any kind of snake in his life, it was too much to have two or even three of the slithering, buzzing reptiles thrown upon the haystack from a single buckrake load of hay. Dan moved on west where fate brought him into the sheep business.

I asked Ben Murphy, the son of Dan, if there was a heritage of sheep raising learned in Ireland. To my surprise, he said, "No, Ireland was a farming and cattle country and sheep played a small part in the economy."

"I guess things were tough in Ireland and the earlier ones to arrive (in the U.S.) would send enough money to pay their fare on a kind of indentured servant thing. They could then work out their debt usually on the terms of the lender."

Dan Murphy was apparently a free man for he soon met a man named Ivan Applegate (a brother of the more famous Captain Applegate) and went to work for him in the sheep business. He admired Applegate and did his work well. According to Ben, "He worked for him first, then Mr. Applegate gave him a band of sheep which he herded and ran for several years, I think maybe three, then they divided them right down the middle. They had some kind of a standard agreement. Somebody who was ambitious and willing to work and really had no capital or backing, was given an opportunity."

52

In this way, ambitious young immigrants joined others who were free to place animals on the open range of Klamath, Lake and Modoc counties.

Before the beginning of Taylor Grazing Permits and Federal Forest Allotments, the sheepmen or cattlemen who got there first were entitled to use the range. Murphy lived the life of a nomad for about eleven years. With no barns, sheds or haystacks, I asked Ben how they wintered the sheep. He replied, "Well, they wintered them in the Lava Beds below Tule Lake. For some reason there isn't as much snow there. Generally they could forage there like the deer do now."

I asked if there was a lot of competition for the wintering ground. Ben said,"I imagine there was but the sheepherders got along pretty well. It wasn't until later that the Tule Lake farmers started putting up hay and selling it to both sheepman and cattlemen to winter herds on. It was at this time that competition really showed up. Some of these haystacks would mysteriously burn up that the sheepherders had bought. Then the same thing started happening to the rest of the hay, so the cows and the sheep were all hungry."

After several years of a nomadic life, the enterprising Murphy purchased the Davis Ranch on the east side of Doublehead Mountain in Modoc County. Taylor grazing and forestry permits provided a more orderly use of the range for summer and winter use. The regulations also provided better protection of the grasslands and forest.

Did this solve the problems of the sheepman? "Only a few," according to Ben. "If you get over 1500 in a band you have forage problems. If the grass is thin it's not practical to have more than that. Some of the bigger operators had several bands but generally we kept them in one band."

By the time Dan Murphy's first son, Ben was born, he could afford to have herders and a camp tender to assist in the operation. Son Ben was permitted at times to live in the sheep camp and share the duties.

Some sheep owners provided the picturesque wagons called "arks" in which to live. The rocky terrain and lack of roads made such vehicles useless around Mt. Doublehead so a tent provided the house and pack animals were used to move the crew.

In utilizing grazing range, the proximity to water was a major problem. "You would take the sheep away from water for two or three days and your donkey had your groceries, your bed and whatever camp outfit....If you abused the burro and could not catch it, you were out there with these sheep and you didn't eat, you didn't have a place to sleep or any water. You were entirely dependent on it.

" The burros could not carry a lot of water so it behooved the sheep herder to conserve as much as he could. He carried a piece of iron or pipe bent into a U-shape and they put that on two rocks. The sagebrush fire below the iron fueled the cooking. They had a coffee pot and a frying pan. Eggs were boiled in the coffee water. Eggs were carried in a coffee can of barley to keep them from breaking. As the eggs were used, we could feed the barley to the donkey. That kept the donkey a little tamer so we could catch it. They roamed with the sheep. You were entirely dependent on them."

Asked if the herders were good cooks, Ben said, "Well, generally they were but the camp tender, when there were two with the band of sheep, did most of the cooking. They were generally good with what they had. A lot took pride in mixing bread in the top of a flour sack. They would add just the right amount of canned milk or water so they got just what they wanted, then they would dip it out and tie the sack until it was needed again."

If the sage brush fire cuisine was tasty and well prepared, apparently the sanitation was somewhat below present day health department standards. Lack of water was a problem. In Ben's words: "This is correct, especially when you are packing it very far. I know when I was a kid, and down there, these shallow lakes like Mud Lake, the cows were wading around in it all the time, and then if you needed water for the camp, you just went out there and dipped it up, and tried

SHEEPHERDER'S ARK—Bryant Williams, long a booster of the sheep industry, stands beside the water and fuel department of an ark. A predecessor of the trailerhouse, these vehicles were popular wherever the range trails permitted their use. Canvas was used for a roof rather than the roofing paper on this one.

to strain the bugs out through your teeth, into a cloth, or whatever. Then streams were pretty scarce out there, so if there was one it would be dug out, and probably lined with boards just like a well. It seemed like these boards would rot and then chipmunks or squirrels or mice would crawl into the well, and it's a wonder we didn't all die of something, but it never seemed to hurt anybody. The only thing was when you dipped this well out dry, you'd find rabbit bones and hair from chipmunks floating around on top of it, and it makes you wonder about it."

The young boy's appetite held up pretty well under most circumstances except during the season when the lambs were docked (tails cut off) and castrated. Then it was a little different. "And some of them used a hot iron to do this, and it kind of seared it and kept the blood from spurting. Generally, it was too much trouble for everybody that I know to do a large bunch of them, so they'd just cut it off. In castrating the male they would just cut the end of this bag off and pull the testicles out with their teeth. This was kind of a standard joke out there too, but this was the way they really did it, and then the same guy who did this would cook the noon meal, or lunch, or whatever it was, and there's nothing less appetizing than to see a guy with dirty hands, and blood all down the front of his shirt or overalls, and come in and cook your lunch without washing his hands, or something like that. This was the way it really happened."

Life on the open range was pretty well regulated by the seasons. The breeding season was regulated by taking the rams by barge onto an island in Tule Lake near the present town of Newell. Highway 39 now cuts through this island. Safe from coyotes and escape, the rams were brought back to the herd for the breeding season.

The most important event was the lambing season usually the middle of March and early April. For centuries domestic sheep have depended somewhat on the help of man in giving birth. There were no barns or lambing sheds. If the weather was bad at Doublehead, the herders would try to drive the sheep to a juniper thicket where the lambs would have some protection from wind, rain and snow. The success of the lambing season was so critical that even the diet of the herders was different. "One thing in the spring when the sheep were lambing, the sheepherders had it much better because they got a lot of canned fruit and all kinds of canned vegetables, pork and beans, things they would not get at other times." Ben explained, "If the lambs don't make it then you're lost for the rest of the year." Obviously, a shepherd with a full stomach felt less likely to leave during the difficult lambing season.

"The owner of a flock of sheep could expect two sources of money during the year- from the sale of lambs and from the wool. Get-

EARLY DAY LAKE COUNTY SHEEP SHEARERS—Large bands of sheep were brought together from Lake County ranges. Hand-operated shears can be seen in the front. Second from right in front row is former County Judge U. E. Reeder.

(Jim Reeder Collection)

ting either to market involved some problems. "Well, this was kind of an experience in itself, because these lambs were generally not in top shape when they came off the summer range, which like I said was around mid or late August. We were then west of Perez and we used to load them at Hackamore, there was a corral there on the Southern Pacific. The lamb buyer usually came from San Francisco or somewhere in California, and he would go out and look at the sheep, and if he thought they were okay, he would set a date to drive them to the corral at the railroad. Early that morning they would run them through a chute, and separate the lambs from the ewes and the smaller lambs, the ones he did not want, and then he would have them sorted out.

"These sheep were probably more like the deer than they were like domestic animals, because like I said, they had never seen the inside of a barn or anything else, and there was no sidetrack or any arrangement there to hold these cars, then you had to wait until the train came. Then it was really something to get these 'wild lambs' into a railroad car. The cars were usually on the head end of the train, right behind the engine, which kept puffing and smoking and making a lot of noise, and it was really something. And then if the train was late, it was even worse trying to do this in the dark. In double-deck cars that you could not stand up in, and trying to get the lambs pushed in there close to this snorting, steaming engine. For awhile we had a goat and he would lead the lambs, they would follow the goat just like another

56

sheep. The goat would run in the door of the car, and make a circle around the car and come back out, and in that time a car was full of lambs, and you could slam the door and pull the goat back out, and you had them in there."

In addition to the horse, burro and Judas goat, the sheep dog, usually the small Australian shepherd, was an essential part of a sheep operation. Since the dogs were trained from the time they were pups, the obedient animals enjoyed working sheep as a hunting dog likes to hunt. My relatives had an old sheep dog that would leave home anytime a band of sheep was driven by.

By railroad, the range-fed lambs were hauled to Bakersfield, California, for fattening.

Shearing and storing wool was another major event. The sheep had to be caught, corraled and clipped. This took place in the middle or latter part of June. In early days the sheep were sheared by hand-powered clippers. When Ben observed the event it was held on the range near Mud Lake in Modoc County. Ben said, "From the time I can remember, they always used all mechanical clippers. They called it a line shaft. They had a long line powered by a one cylinder gas engine. The individual shearer had a clutch arrangement so that he could turn his clippers on or off individually. We would have eight, ten, or twelve shearers work at once."

The range animals were first put in a large corral, then a smaller one, finally into a bin so the shearers could catch and hold them to remove the fleece.

Sheepshearing is an exhausting and difficult job. Holding the animal requires special technique. These men would start in southern California and they would gradually work northward clear to Montana. Paid by the head, they kept count by the number of strings used to tie the wool.

If you have never seen a wool sack, it would be hard to under-stand how large they are. Taller than a man, the sacks required a special method for filling. Ben explained, "There was a stand kind of thing and then one man, kid or whoever would stay in the sack and keep stomping the wool down. You could get about 250 pounds. Then you could raise it with a pole with a kind of lever effect to get the weight off the bottom. You make an ear on each corner of the bottom, then the top, so a couple of men could drag it around and roll it up. In June, when shearing was done, it is usually nice weather but at other times it gets sultry with a thunderstorm and heavy rain. These sacks were laying out there and then this wool would take on water. Instead of having a 200 pound sack, you would have a 500-600 pound sack.

"The wool was hauled on wagons but in the early days there were no railroads and the roads were real rough and hard on the wooden

WOOL SACKS—Giant size burlap sacks were used to hold the wool ready for transport.

wheeled wagons. At one tme, they loaded the wool onto rafts or barges about where Highway 39 comes out of the Tule Lake basin. They then poled the craft around Tule Lake and up Lost River to unload at Merrill. The dock there was just south of the bridge."

Getting the wool and selling it at a profit were two different things. Ben said in his time "they would take the wool to the home ranch at Henley and sell it to a buyer who would haul it to the railroad. In the depression during the 30's, my dad kept the wool for several years, then the sacks rotted and we had to resack it. Finally the several years accumulation sold for five or six cents a pound which is not very much."

Sheep camp life had its happy times as well as some very bad times. One of the worst occasions for the Murphys was in 1936 as described by Ben. "Now you hear of these blizzards and they are dropping bales of hay to animals. Once I can remember we got caught out at Doublehead which is about ten miles from the highway. There was no way to get the sheep out of there. The snow was probably three or four feet deep. They made a kind of V-shaped thing out of planks. The horses pulled this through the snow to make a kind of ditch, then the sheep would follow along behind. We lost several hundred sheep that winter bringing them the ten miles from Doublehead Mountain to the overpass on the highway at Perez. We couldn't even feed them hay." An exhausting and emotional trip.

For a man from the green of Ireland, life on the rocky, sagelands of Modoc County must have been dull and boring. Ben related, "Well, my dad said that really early, when he was working with the Applegates, down there south of the Lava Beds somewhere, he was packing through there with several pack-horses, going out to take supplies to one of these herders. He came to a cave with a hole in the ground down there, kind of a sink-thing. He tied the horses up to a tree there, and took a rope and dropped it down this hole down into the cave, and he had a pine knot for a torch and he was looking around in the cave. At that time, he probably hadn't seen anyone out there for a month. But while he was down in the cave one of the cowboys from the D-Ranch over by Dorris came through there looking for strays, or just riding through. He thought it would be a good joke so he pulled the rope up. Then when my dad got tired of looking around this cave, he decided he would come out and the rope was gone. He decided he'd have to do something or he would die there. So he started picking up loose rocks, and trying to build some sort of a stairstep or some way he could get up this vertical wall so he could get out the opening. Finally the guy on top decided that he had had enough so he threw the rope down. I don't know what kind of remarks were exchanged when he got out.

Ben related another experience that his father had, "In this same area down towards Medicine Lake, he was camped there with some sheep in the summer. An eagle had a nest up in one of the pine trees, a big nest out on a limb, and for some reason he decided that he wanted to see what was in the nest. He shot the limb with a rifle and the weight of the nest caused the nest to fall down and there was a young eagle in it. Then he felt kind of badly about this. It wasn't an endangered species then or anything, but he really had no intention of harming the eagle. So he built a rock pen with a brush top on it, and then on through the summer, he raised this eagle until it was big enough to fly. He said the eagle would stand back there and catch these hard sourdough biscuits in his mouth. He would open his mouth and catch one of them when you would throw it to him. That and lamb meat or venison were fed to this bird. Finally that fall when he was done, he took the top off the pen and the eagle was able to fly away and off on his own. He was raised on a sheepherder's diet." Chalk up one victory for the Audubon Society-an eagle with an Irish accent who could catch a curve thrown with a sourdough biscuit.

In the Klamath country sheep raising has changed greatly since the open range days. Antibiotics, grain and hay pellets, truck transportation and federal land laws have all served to stabilize the sheep industry. There are, however, descendants of the early Irish who continue in the sheep business. The wily coyotes who howled their mournful messages to the sheep dogs continue to thrive and prey upon the sheep even into the fringes of civilization.

BILL KITTREDGE
COWBOY - CATTLEMAN

The setting: East of Table Mountain in northern Lake County lies a wide, level, sage-covered plain punctuated by ridges that once marked the shores of Pleistocene lakes. The plain extends past Christmas Valley on to Wagontire Mountain in Harney County. It was on this plain and surrounding juniper hills that the small independent cattlemen of the region allowed their animals to feed. The bunchgrass would support horses even in the winter months. There was very little deeded land or fenced area and no government supervision. It was called "open range."

Each year livestock owners would join to round up the animals in order to brand the offspring with the brand of the mother.

The scene: Several branding irons are heating in a small open fire. Horsemen bring in the colts, one man tends the irons, others rope and tie the colts. As a tall cattleman is about to apply the iron, another challenges the ownership of the horse. This man is Linc Hutton, known to be a dangerous man. He is wearing a gun now. The stockman rises from the captive colt and approaches Hutton. Suddenly the cowboy tending the fire seizes a red hot iron and holding it close to the face of Hutton said, "If you go for your gun, you'll get this iron in your face." This courageous man was Charlie Howard. He had saved the life of the colt's young owner, Bill Kittredge.

The father of Bill Kittredge had been a gold miner coming around Cape Horn to California in 1849. He had received seminary training and was teaching in an Indian school in Washington Territory when son Bill was born in 1876 in Yakima County, Washington.

The family moved to a homestead near Silver Lake in 1888. Son Bill did such work as was available, driving four horse freight teams to Shaniko, a rail-head town, trailing cattle herds to both Shaniko and Gazelle, California, another rail-head town.

At about the time of the Spanish American War, a Silver Lake rancher, Jim Small, signed a contract to deliver a large herd of cavalry horses to Lincoln, Nebraska. Young Bill was hired for trail boss. He, with four other buckaroos, was to drive the animals over the torturous route and deliver them to the government. Such an assignment would seem impossible. They had to swim the horses across the Snake River and from there they pretty much followed the Old Oregon Trail.

Their supplies were hauled by horseteam on a buckboard. In the rainy weather, they took turns enjoying the luxury of sleeping under the buckboard. They also took turns "nighthawking." This was the duty of guarding the herd at night and while on horseback keeping the

WHEN HORSEPOWER WAS "HORSE POWER"—Teams of horses traveling in a circular motion turned the power mechanism which was transmitted by a steel rod to the threshing machine. The horses patiently stepped over the rod in making each trip.

(Jim Reeder collection)

herd together. After this nerve-wracking but successful trek, Bill returned to Silver Lake.

He rented a place there and while still working part time for others, bought a few cows and was in the stock business for himself. In 1899 he met a Corvallis girl, Maude Long, who was visiting the Lanes. They were married and had three children: Oscar Kittredge born in 1900; Marie, mother of my informant, Donovan Nicol, was born in 1903; Vi Gouldin, the second daughter, was born in 1905.

As time passed, Bill's herd grew and more land was needed. Pasture land on the Klamath Marsh was first rented and then in 1914 the land there was purchased. Deep snow made the marsh ranch usable only in the summer so a ranch in the north end of Summer Lake was purchased to provide an irrigated place to grow hay. Gradually land claims on the Klamath Marsh were bought until his holdings there reached 12,500 acres.

In the late 1920's, Kittredge rented the Sodhouse Ranch in Harney County. The large cattle trucks were not available so the long trail ride between ranches became an annual event. Cowboys, accompanied by a chuck wagon, moved the herds slowly across the rocky and, in some places, mountainous desert. Stops were planned at various springs where horses and cattle could obtain water.

The buckaroos knew their business and took good care of the animals but on one occasion they stayed overnight in a place where the poisonous weed larkspur was growing. Jack said that so many cattle died after eating the larkspur that his grandfather just about went broke.

Getting the cattle to market at a railroad sometimes meant drives of 150 to 180 miles, sometimes to Shaniko and sometimes to Gazelle, California. Later rails were extended to Crane in Harney

HARVEST SEASON AT SILVER LAKE—Neighbors in the Silver Lake homestead community gathered to thresh grain. The straw was carried to the stack by a conveyor rather than a blower. Jim Reeder is the sack sewer at the lower right.

County and still later to Kirk in Klamath County north of Chiloquin.

In 1929 Kittredge received word that the MC Ranch in Warner Valley was for sale. He looked at it but could not finance it, but in the 1930's money was raised for the purchase of this enormous ranch. About this time, the U.S. Government bought the main part of the Pete French ranch for a bird refuge. This enabled Bill to buy the range land which included a spring for cattle water.

The son of a miner who started at the bottom by this time had purchased and developed the largest family-owned cattle empire in the west. It included 24,000 acres of irrigated land; 36,000 total of deeded land in ownership; with BLM leased range it totaled 850,000 acres.

At the MC Ranch in Warner Valley, Jack said that it required 24 horse drawn mowers and 10 dump rakes to bunch the hay. Most of it was brought to the stackyards with buckrakes and laid on rope nets. These nets were then lifted with a tall wooden derrick by horse power. The hay was then dropped from the nets and the men on the stack would place it with pitchforks so that it would remain dry enough and not spoil.

Feeding was then done in the winter months from horse drawn hay wagons. Another method of feeding was used by simply bunching up the hay in piles by buckrakes, then allowing the cattle in to feed while the weather was still dry enough to keep the hay from spoiling. The ranch kept about 400 horses for their farming operation to provide the 7,000 cows, plus their calves, with food.

62

BILL KITTREDGE—In his favorite place on a horse with his cattle. He was Oregon's first and only one elected to the Cowboy Hall of Fame.

(Wesley Guderian photo)

Nicol said that his grandfather was always on the move. A new ranch meant a move to a different house. Once a nice house was built but they lived in it only two years. When I asked for pictures, few were available. "They would spend a lot of time taking pictures, of a squirrel, a bull or a bird but cared little for pictures of themselves." according to Jack.

Since the Klamath Marsh ranch was on the Klamath Indian Reservation, I asked the grandson how they got along with their Indian neighbors. "Fine," he said, "They liked them." In the early days there, on one occasion they moved into a cabin when the Indian moved out.

One story Bill Kittredge told was about a grizzly bear hunt on the Summer Lake Rim. A group of cowboys was trying to get a big grizzly that had been killing cattle. Finally they had some shots at the bear which took refuge in a small cave. Each hunter was anxious to be the one who finished the last grizzly bear but none wanted to enter the cave. Finally, one of the Indians, a Paiute, was persuaded to enter the cave with a long pole and spook the bear out. He entered and chased the bear out and it was promptly shot by the other Indian leaving the buckaroos with little to brag about.

SECOND ANNUAL PRODUCTION CREDIT MEETING—The directors invited 4-H club members to their meeting. Many now are successful farmers and businessmen. Lee McMullen and Ray Michels were managers of the bank in this year.

(Kennell Ellis photo)

Jack said, "Kittredge was a developer, a reclaimer and had great dedication to improving cattle breeds." He always wanted the best bulls and stallions. At the time of his death there were 20,000 head of cattle.

Big dreams took big money, sometimes more than banks had to offer. This was the case during the depression of the 1930's. At this time, Bill Kittredge and others took advantage of a new federal program to establish a Production Credit Bank owned and operated by the borrowers. Lee McMullen was hired as secretary and an association was formed. Among the first directors were : A. R. Campbell, Gene Hammond and U. E. Reeder. Kittredge, who was fondly called "Bill Kit" by his friends, was elected president. The organization served the needs well and still remains sound and active today when many financial institutions are in stress.

In Oklahoma City on Persimmon Hill there was established a Cowboy Hall of Fame. Two cattlemen were Oregon's first nominees to be elected: the famous Pete French and Bill Kittredge. So far as we know they are the only Oregonians to be so honored.

When you ride through the town of Silver Lake toward Lakeview, you will see picturesque Table Mountain before you. About five miles out there is a bridge where the waters from the former Paulina Marsh went into Silver Lake. On your left toward the north lie the juniper-covered Connelly Hills. In this basin is where the son of a miner and teacher got his start toward becoming Oregon's biggest cattleman.

64

LIFE ABOARD A LAKE BOAT

If you have never ridden behind a team of horses, you cannot truly appreciate the value of the early day boats that served the lakes and rivers of the Klamath country. The roads were always bumpy and sometimes muddy. The wagons and buckboards of the early 1900's were constructed for stout, and not for comfort. Even the finest buggies lacked the springs and shock absorbers that we take for granted on our present-day vehicles.

The second disadvantage of horse-drawn vehicles was the time which it took an ordinary horse team to travel. I remember as a child, it seemed that it took forever to travel the three miles to visit my mother's friend at the Cochran Creek Ranch. Winter travel was sometimes made more comfortable with hot bricks at your feet or one of the new-fangled oilburning foot warmers.

Horse lovers like the smell of horses, but the average early day traveler only tolerated the various odors emanating from the snorting dobbins. Most teams were well-behaved, but even the best required a driver who understood them, and the various machines and animals that might spook them and cause a runaway.

It's easy to understand why travelers entering the Klamath country by stagecoach at Keno, Teeter's Landing or Ady were glad to make the change from horse-power to a steamboat. It is also understandable why early resorts such as Harriman Lodge and the resort at Eagle Ridge were built to be accommodated by water transportation.

Certainly of greater importance and more widespread use of boats was the transportation of commodities. One man who took an

The ramp at Eagle Landing where sand was unloaded. The Eagle is at dockside; in the background is the more modern Modoc. The latter was used to push barges in Upper Lake commerce.

active part in water transportation was J.P. (Jack) Linman. He provid-
ed much of the information on steamboating on Klamath Lake. Young
Jack was eight years old when the Linman family moved to Klamath
Falls and lived near Pelican Marina.

Linman can be said to have come into his marine knowledge by
heritage. His father was John Albert Linman born in Sweden in 1865.
He was conscripted into the Swedish navy. The young sailor jumped
ship in Liverpool, England, without knowing a single word of English.
He then worked as a seaman until 1890 and later entered shipyard
work in Alameda, California. He was married in San Francisco to Mary
Cannon.

While working in the shipyards of Alameda, John Albert Linman
met another man of Nordic descent named Wickstrom. In 1910, they
formed a partnership, came to Klamath Falls and constructed a barge-
type boat which they named "The Eagle." It had a steam tractor
engine with a chain-drive to the paddle wheel but had no reverse gear.
It had to be shoved from shore by hand and landed in the same way.
The Eagle was used principally to transport sand from the Williamson
River to the dock called Eagle Landing at Klamath Falls. It took one
day for The Eagle to leave Klamath and arrive at the Williamson River.
When it arrived, they would shift the chain over from the paddle wheel
to a pump, and they would pump the sand on board. It took a day to
load the craft. The next day was spent on the way to Klamath Falls.
They would cross the lake above Bare Island to Eagle Ridge. They
then followed the deep water down the Skillet Handle. After coming to
McCornack Point, they would go over toward the dock at Klamath
Falls. After they arrived there, the barge would be unloaded using
wheelbarrows to wheel the sand up a ramp where they dumped it onto
horse-drawn wagons. The wagons would then transport the sand to
the various places in Klamath Falls where it was used in making cement and plaster.

The crew of the Eagle slept on bunks and took turns acting as
"cook." Jack said that the food was wholesome but not fancy. One of
the great problems, of course, was sleeping overnight on the Williamson River. In the summer the mosquitoes were terrific. In order to
sleep, the crew would burn green leaves in 5-gallon cans to try to keep
the mosquitoes away. The smoke from burning of the leaves was
sometimes worse than the mosquitoes so they would have to give up.

About the only visitors the sand loaders would have on the river
would be an occasional Indian woman in a log dugout canoe seeking
to trade fish for tobacco. The ladies did not care whether it was chew-
ing tobacco, cigars, or loose pipe variety.

The operation of the canoes seemed simple enough for the native
American ladies so one day when an empty dugout came drifting by,

LINMAN WITH BROAD AXE
—The ship's timbers on the early boats were hand-hewn with a wood axe and other hand tools. This photo shows Jack Linman with the broadaxe used by his father in boat building.

Jack Linman and a fellow boat crewman decided to take a joy ride. It turned out to be a swim. They were hardly away from the shore when Jack said that the boat threw them. The palefaces were never able to operate the dugout successfully. They wondered how the natives were able to stay afloat on the choppy waves of Upper Klamath Lake.

There were many fish in the Williamson River at that time. Jack and his partner would fish without a pole trolling with a hand-line. Instead of fishing in the river proper, they would troll off the mouth of the river where the river water entered the lake. The water of the lake would sometimes get very rough with the high waves driven by the wind but The Eagle had a draft of 4½ feet, so that the waves apparently did not affect it. Jack never recalled having to layover because of bad weather.

About 1915, suppliers started bringing in Mt. Shasta sand on the railroad and this proved to be a little better for the making of concrete. However, the plasterers preferred the Williamson River sand because it had a slight content of pumice.

During the process of the sand business, Mr. Wickstrom and Mr. Linman built a companion boat called "The Modoc." It was a tugboat type, whereas "The Eagle" had been a barge. In 1912, both boats burned. Mr. Wickstrom rebuilt both of them a little later. By 1915, Captain Linman bought a boiler and some stern-wheel type engines that had been designed for marine use from Tom Calmes, who had

KLAMATH DUGOUT CANOE—Indian women were expert at rowing this craft. This is the long deep water type. Smaller craft was used for gathering wocas and duck eggs.

Captain John A. Linman looks from the pilothouse of the Wasp while son, Jack, stands below.

been running a boat on Tule Lake. Linman mounted these engines on a boat called "The Wasp." With this boat, he towed logs from the Williamson River and the various other loading places on the Upper Lake and he also hauled cinders from a place called Coon Point. He sold The Wasp to the power company in 1927. He then rented the boat "The Canby" from Thomas McCormick and towed logs from Keno to the Ackley Mill on Lake Ewauna at Klamath Falls.

The Klamath Queen, another craft that played an important part in the building of the Klamath country, was a large dredge used to build the railroad grade along the shore of the lake. E. P. McCornack bought The Klamath Queen after the railroad work was finished, and he used it to build the dike to reclaim the Caledonia Marsh, which we have known as the Geary Ranch. Jack Linman worked as a roustabout on the crew of the Klamath Queen. One of his jobs was to bring the launch downtown in order to get fuel and supplies for The Klamath Queen.

Tule Lake proved a waterway for the hauling of such commodities as cinders and also for wool. I know in one instance, wool was hauled across Tule Lake, up Lost River, and unloaded at Merrill. Wood also, and hay, were hauled on Tule Lake and the Lower Klamath Lake by early boat operators.

There were two different steamboats owned by my wife's grandfather, Thomas McCormick of Keno. His first boat purchased from a man named Dusenberry was called "The Mayflower." It was driven with a rope belt from the steam engine to the paddle wheel. McCormick used it mainly to haul lumber from the sawmill that he owned at Keno. "The Canby" also a steamboat was one of the few boats in operation for both freight and passenger traffic. My wife's father, U. E. Reeder, who later became county judge, was the operator for McCormick on both The Mayflower and The Canby. The cement used in the construction of the Klamath Irrigation District dam and tunnel was hauled from Laird's Landing on Lower Klamath Lake up to Klamath Falls.

Judge Reeder told me that in the management of the boat navigation was only part of the problem. He said that the crew, which sometimes consisted of relatives, also required careful supervision. One of the varieties of cargo moving from the landing at Keno to Klamath Falls was barrels of bar whiskey. Since the liquor was contained in wooden kegs, the boat roustabouts would remove the wooden plugs from the kegs and siphon out what they considered a fair share. They would replace the contents with water.

Another trial in managing the crew was to hold down on the practical jokes during the dull moments of the upriver voyage. One person who was evidently the victim of a practical joke was Henry Boivin.

Henry, who was the father of Senator Harry Boivin, owned the only plumbing shop and steamfitting license in Klamath Falls. On one occasion, he was called to make repairs on the steam pipes of The Canby. In order to get even with the jokesters of the crew, he plumbed steam into the boat's only toilet. When the first member of the crew went in to use the facility, it was so rigged that the steam shot out when the chain was pulled to flush the toilet. The story goes that young Tom McCormick took the door off the toilet room as he left the seat.

Apparently, Henry was an accomplished jokester himself. He was a member of the Ashland Elks Lodge at one time, and in order to start a lodge in Klamath Falls, he organized what he called an "Antlers Club." When the members of the Klamath Falls Antlers Club went to Ashland in order to take part in their official initiation, Boivin apparently took advantage of the power of his position in that ceremony. He must have given some of the local men a pretty rough time. So when the good brothers came back on the stage from Ashland and arrived in Keno, the victims of the abuse got together and strapped Boivin on a board and loaded him into The Canby for the ride to Klamath Falls. Having called ahead, they were met at the wharf by the hearse of the town's undertaker, Earl Whitlock. The board on which Mr. Boivin was strapped was then taken to the funeral parlor where he was placed in a position of prominence and grace. Harry said that the next morning his mother went down and cut Henry away from the board on which he was strapped.

The building of the railroad about 1909-1910, closed off the channel between the Klamath River and Lower Klamath Lake and effectively stopped the use of the Lower Lake for boat transportation. This, of course, meant the Laird's Landing was no longer usable. The construction of the railroad rather effectively did away with most of the freight business on the waterways of the Klamath country. Excursion boats and recreation uses continued with various types of boats, including The Winema, but generally speaking public transportation by boat ended. Now, of course, there is heavy use of boating by the individual owners of the recreation craft.

An additional value has been found in the waters of the Upper Lake. A nutritional supplement is being made from the recovery and processing of algae.

IDA MOMYER—About the age of 17, a
student at the Ashland Normal School.

IDA ODELL - TINY TIGER

Henry Momyer, who had operated small retail stores in other places, obtained a license from the federal government under $10,000 bond to act as Post Indian Trader at the Klamath Indian Agency. The percentage of profit and types of commodities were closely regulated by Indian Service rules. In 1899, daughter Ida arrived at the Agency to help her father in the store.

On one particular snowy winter day, her father and brother Harry were both out of town and she was operating the store by herself. Two young Indians, Blaine Ben John and Gordon Miller had the reputation of being bad boys. They had been hanging around the store for quite some time when they approached her saying, "What you do if we rob you?" Ida was less than five feet tall and weighed under 100 pounds. She reached under the counter and grasped her father's cheese knife and held it out in a threatening way. She said, "Both boys laughed

71

ALEX MARTIN—Founder of the Old Brick Store and adjacent Klamath State Bank.

heartily at my bluff but, just the same, after that those two young rascals were the first to greet me each morning and took upon themselves the sweeping of the floor, carrying wood and doing errands for me."

The courage of this delicate and sensitive woman was tested many times, at least twice when she was serving as city treasurer. On one occasion, she stood up to the city council and clerk in refusing to allow them to use monies earmarked for repaving South 6th Street, to pay off city bonds.

On another occasion, she faced down two state bank examiners who were demanding turnover of warrants held for security. G. C. Lorenz had taken a contract to construct a sewer line and for security on a loan to finance the project, had agreed to assign warrant payments to the city. The warrants were good but the First Trust Bank had closed its doors permanently. Ida told of her problems:

"A young examiner by the name of Hooper was sent by the State Banking Department to liquidate the institution. One day he and another State examiner walked up to my window and formally requested the return of the city warrants. I told him I would be glad to trade the warrants for the city money on deposit there. They told me I knew quite well they couldn't do that. They went on to point out according to State Law it was illegal for me to have these warrants as security. Although shaking in my shoes, I still refused to part with the securities. We always kept a set of the Oregon Codes, and after they had gone I looked up the statute. This was clear in its wording that it was illegal <u>for a bank</u> to secure deposits of a municipality by giving their assets as security. In the afternoon the two State men came and again demanded the Warrants and again referred to the State Law. I was still quite shaky over my predicament, but did call their attention to the wording of the law wherein nothing was written making it illegal for a municipal officer to accept security, the illegality being only on the part of the institution which gave it. It happened that on the day this demand was made on the City Treasurer, National Bank Examiners were working in our place. One of these men, Arthur James, and I were quite good friends. I was really worried and went to Arthur and told him the whole story asking if he had any suggestions. Arthur said, "Ida, where are these warrants?" and I told him I had them in the vault. All he said was, "Don't you think that's a fine place for them?"

No further demands for the warrants were made until Arthur Wilson became mayor and the warrants were called for redemption.

What kind of background could generate in this young lady such determination and such a sense of justice? Ida was born in the Pennsylvania coal region on December 24, 1881 to a mother who had high moral standards and was an excellent disciplinarian. Her father apparently had great self-assurance and a strong urge for adventure. Both parents joined in teaching Ida and her brother arithmetic by playing cribbage with them.

The family moved from Pennsylvania, first to Oakland, later to Red Bluff. While Momyer owned a store in the East, he was also trained as a carpenter. What was described as "itchy feet" caused the family to make several moves before coming to Oregon in 1895.

They settled in a home south of Merrill where the children could attend the Gale School. Ida explained, "When we first came to Oregon, we lived in California." (Their home south of Merrill was across the stateline.) From this place, Henry's shotgun and the millions of waterfowl provided meat for the table and feathers for pillows and ticks (mattresses).

Nate Merrill discovered that wheat could be grown successfully in the valley so a flour mill was built by Martin and Brandon to mill their Anchor Brand flour. When the Momyers arrived, the town consisted only of the flour mill, the bridge across Lost River and Jim O'Farrell's Grocery Store.

The population center then was at Gale where they rode horseback to school. As the population shifted toward Merrill, the post office was moved there from Gale. Henry Momyer became the new postmaster and built a livery barn and stocked a general merchandise store.

Young Ida, who now lived in back of the store, would help rush to the clothes line to remove the flapping sheets when cowboys warned them not to stampede the hundreds of cattle which moved through the town on the trail to Montague or Ager. She would sit on the counter of her father's store and listen to the stories of Jesse Carr's cowboys with wide-eyed interest.

At Merrill, Momyer and the other people in the new town, raised money by subscription and built a school. This board and bat structure also, on Sunday, served as a church for the Dunkard faith. The first teacher was J. G. Fairclo, an expert pensman and artist.

When Ida was seventeen, the itchy feet of her father led to moving the merchandise from Merrill to the Klamath Agency. She described her life there, "There was little time for idleness. A meal meant much preparation. All bread home baked, and, of course, cakes, cookies and pies were made from scratch - pies often from dried fruit. All washing was with a zinc washboard, water heated in a tin and copper boiler - and there is one in my basement now. As the only utility room we had was the unenclosed back porch, washing in winter was not my favorite sport. Many sheets from the three to four beds were scrubbed to a whiteness which rivaled the snow beneath them where they hung, frozen stiff, from their rope lines. We wore many white petticoats all starched to a stand-by-yourselfness. Great baskets of ironing were done, always on Tuesdays. Mother's schedule varied for no reasons. There just were no reasons why the washing should not be on the line Monday morning, the ironing and the clothes put away on Tuesday. Wednesday was probably baking day. The house was clean-

AGENCY BASEBALL TEAM—These players provided skilled opposition to any teams in the Basin at that time. **(Odell Collection)**

74

ed each day, but at least once a week every piece of furniture was moved and the floors broom swept. Kitchen was scrubbed - not mopped - it was a hands and knees job with a scrub brush and soft soap.

"The ride to Klamath Falls in winter was long and cold. We had little, carpet-covered metal foot warmers which were filled with red hot briquets when we started and remained warm the entire thirty-two miles. These were put at our feet and under the coyote skin robe which mother had made from the furs and lined with soft flannelette and we were quite cozy, but how good the lights of the little town looked as we finally reached the summit of what you know as O.T.I. hill, and that name will soon be a memory along with many other memories. If we got in early enough, it was interesting to see the many steam jets rising along the flat and side hill as we drove down the long grade."

The Ashland Normal School was a popular place for Klamath County students in the early 1900's. Enrolled there from the Agency were Ida Momyer, Clara and Kay Loosley and Leta Nickerson. From the Williamson River Mission in attendance was Frances Beatty, daughter of Reverend Beatty after whom the town of Beatty was named.

There were two dormitories but Ida said that it was not easy for the President B. F. Mulkey to arrange to feed the boarding students. They ate in the basement and helped by waiting on tables and washing dishes.

Traveling to and from the Normal School to the Agency by stagecoach, boat and railroad were sometimes unsought adventures. On one occasion she wrote after staying overnight in the Linkville Hotel: "The next morning we dressed in our icy room, broke the ice on the water pitcher, washed in the big crockery bowl and after breakfast walked to the nearby dock and got on the little boat which was to take us to Keno where a four-horse stage would get us over the mountain. Less than three miles down the Klamath River ice had cut into the boat's hull to such an extent that we had to turn back and at the Linkville Hotel a team and light rig came and drove merrily, if somewhat frozenly, off for Keno. There we were put on a stage and set on our way. On one of these trips in warmer weather Ethel and I were taken by Pokegama where a logging railroad connected with the Southern Pacific. The "coaches" were box cars with benches along the sides. After the rough stage rides these old box cars were unheard of luxury. A fine old spring at Potter's Mill induced a stop so we could all quench a real or imaginary thirst out of a common tin dipper which hung on the flume.

"On another trip returning to school in the winter over the snowy Greenspring, going down the icy grade the four horses decided to run

HENRY MOMYER—The first Crater Lake National Park ranger to wear a uniform.

(Odell Collection)

away. We went thundering down those slippery wheel tracks until the leaders stumbled and fell, which stopped the wheel horses. Lynn Yaden, the driver, got the horses untangled and we resumed the trip."

In 1904 the Agency Store was sold to Orville and J. Russell Elliott. The Momyer family moved to San Francisco where Henry had found a location for a grocery store. As luck would have it, Ida was there for the San Francisco earthquake and she describes her experience: "In 1906 · April 18th, came the devastating earthquake and fire and I sat on the summit of Lone Cross Mountain and watched our city burn. I have seen many accounts of this fire, but none have been able to describe it, nor can I. The raging flames would start at one end of a Market Street block and literally before you could draw a deep breath that block was gone and another under attack. When the firefighters started dynamiting buildings before the fire could reach them, it was finally brought under control at the lower side of Van Ness Avenue. This was a very wide street of magnificent homes. Its width was helpful in controlling the fire. When the smoke cleared away, department stores such as the Emporium, Hales Bros., etc. formerly on Market Street rented the spacious grounds in front of the palatial homes and in no time had built wooden stores and started up in business. I have a picture of the Emporium in its new frame building.

SUPERINTENDENT'S OFFICE—Crater Lake National Park headquarters about 1908.
(Odell Collection)

We took pictures of everything. As you know, the city was under military rule for a while. General Funston was in command at the Presidio and put in charge of the city. Armed soldiers patrolled our streets to restrain looting, to watch that gas lights were not used or cooking fires built in the residences. Gas mains were broken and a new fire could start anywhere and broken water mains offered no protection."

Following the earthquake, the Momyers did not try to reestablish their business. Ida took a job as a presser in the alteration department of a large store on Market Street. Here she learned to cope with the traffic and customs of San Francisco.

A friend told her that she should learn to be a secretary so she bought some books and rented an old Remington typewriter. Attending business school evenings, she walked home from the streetcar on Geary street, and sometimes ran, keeping clear of dark sidewalks and recessed house entrances. After quitting her first job, she worked as head stenographer for a firm publishing law books, Bender Moss. She received good pay, $40 per month, later raised to $50.

Regardless of this success, the girl who had grown up at Merrill and Klamath Agency found living in the rebuilding of the city difficult. She wrote, "Noise around us was nerve shattering. Every salvageable brick was having mortar ground off and these machines were everywhere. Great mechanized hammers were riveting huge steel frames with ear-piercing clamer. Sanitary conditions in San Francisco were bad for some time. Ships docking in the bay from the Orient carried rats infected with bubonic plague. The ruins made ideal cover for them."

The opportunity finally came for Ida to return to the Klamath Country. Her father Henry had been working at Crater Lake National Park and in 1908 had moved back to Klamath Falls. He told Mr. E. R. Reames of Ida's desire to work there. Alex Martin, cashier and manager of the Klamath County Bank, sent word that she could go to work immediately.

In 1909 the trip was easier. She took the Southern Pacific train which now went as far as Weed, then a little stub line to Ady. The rest of the trip was by steamboat up the Klamath River and the boat landed at "Cap" Wilkins' dock near the bridge on the shore of Lake Ewauna.

In the state-chartered bank, Alex Martin, Jr. was assisted by Leslie Rogers and A. R. (Orb) Campbell. On the board of directors were Rufus Moore and C. S. Moore, who later became state treasurer. An arch opened between the bank and the "Old Brick Store" located at Main and Conger. A competing bank, First National operated up the street under a national charter.

Ida said Alexander Martin, Sr. was a beloved character. In addition to banking, he would play the fiddle for dances in Jacksonville for the miners in the early days. Most borrowers would arrange for credit in advance but some insisted in running over-drafts. The State Banking Department took a dim view of this way of doing business calling attention to the fact that it was "unbusiness-like, undesirable, also illegal." The director gave instructions to eliminate over-drafts. Then Alexander Martin, Sr. instructed these over-draft checks to be run over Ida's window and the money taken from his personal account. She was instructed to total the balance each month, then charge 10% monthly interest.

The security rules were somewhat different from the present. Ida wrote, "Coming to our community from the Alaskan gold fields and settling at Fort Klamath, where they built and operated a sawmill, were Frank Burns and J. W. Utter. These fine men brought back a buckskin bag of nuggets, almost pure gold.

"In those days there were few safety deposit boxes and customers' tin boxes were stacked high in our vault. These were ordinary tin cash boxes and practically all keys were interchangeable. Customers kept their papers and valuables in them and we handed out a box when wanted.

"Utter and Burns kept their buckskin bag with their nuggets in such a box with their papers. Among the nuggets was one as large as the palm of my hand (fingers excluded) about the shape of my palm, in places almost as thick. It was heavy, it was interesting in those careless, trusting days not one of us ever hesitated to drag out that bag of nuggets and to exhibit this big one to an admiring audience and Utter and Burns wouldn't think of locking the box and depriving us of this

LAKESIDE INN—The men about town ready for a ride. The man in the derby hat is Senator George Baldwin. Where are the ladies? (Odell Collection)

pleasure."

The bank managers found as time passed that their former stenographer had unusual talent. Her responsibilities increased and she was made assistant cashier. Among other assignments, she was sent out to collect on overdue loans. It seems hard to imagine the tiny woman as a bill collector but she apparently met with success.

The Klamath County Bank's board of directors wanted the name "national" in the title so bought out the First National Bank. The building it had occupied was converted into the Hall Hotel by E. B. Hall.

Ida found the Klamath Falls environment considerably better than San Francisco but it was not without drawbacks. She wrote, "At the time the banks moved from the river our streets were a mess. When I lived at 7th and Oak, winter streets when not frozen, were a sea of mud. Women wore street length skirts and it was simply impossible to keep the hems free from mud. I kept a pair of shoes at the bank and wore knee length rubber boots to work. At night I would hang my skirt behind the stove and when the bottom dried, I'd take it in both hands and rub the fabric together to loosen up the mud for brushing.

"In 1912 my father, mother and I pooled our scant resources and bought the dwelling at 228 Juniper, now Ewauna Street. At that time, the Ankeny Ditch prowled around town. It wound around the brow of the ridge which forms the embankment above Conger, and took its unhurried way down Pine in front of Bess Hunt's. Juniper Street dropped down to main by means of a long flight of wooden stairs. Water snakes found the Ankeny Ditch a pleasant addition to their habitat, but were frequently impelled to seek Lake Ewauna and Link River, and when this impulse and my travels to work coincided, it was not too funny. If you can picture a lady in long skirts descending a stairway with a snake popping out from under the step she is just about to use, you will get the idea. The sidewalk along Main was feet above street level, was made of boards laid lengthwise with wide cracks between. Out of these cracks, busy little reptiles slithered through and went hurriedly about their business, adding no happiness to my long trudge. The wooden sidewalks followed the street level by stairs ascending and descending in conformity to the little hills. Worse then the snakes were the frog migrations from Lake Ewauna to Upper Klamath. These frogs were tiny fellows about as big as the end of the thumb and there were so many that you simply could not walk without stepping on them. Marie McMillan, whose mother owned the Lakeside Inn for years, told me that she had walked to the stores carrying a broom to sweep them out from in front of her."

In August of 1917, Ida resigned her position as assistant cashier at the First National Bank and, after working for a brief time at Crater Lake, was offered the job as cashier at a new bank being formed. The new bank under a state charter was called the Klamath State Bank. A new building was to be constructed at 6th and Main Street. During the period of construction, Ida was asked to serve as secretary to a sheep raising partnership called Tryon and McKendree. The small office she occupied here became, in addition to the sheep headquarters, the bank cashier's office, and school clerk's office as she had been school clerk for some years.

Mr. McKendree bought about 20,000 head of breeding ewes and formed partnerships with six different partners who were to attend the sheep on a share basis. This enterprise opened up a new chapter in the life of Ida B. as the sheepmen called her. There was both joy and tragedy in the assignment. She said the bookkeeping was weird as the partners were always trading among themselves. Her duties included measuring haystacks, counting sheep and even getting the herders out of jail. Conflict over shearing corrals, water holes and open range was a constant reality. Eventually O. T. McKendree was murdered.

Ida eventually got into the sheep business for herself. She said that "Along with my father, I bought a small band of ewes. It doesn't take a band of ewes long to double in number when no "she" stuff is sold. One of the nuisances of this is having to run a dry band. What changed conditions I saw in the three years the lease lasted! The second winter we bought hay between Adams Point and Malin and then trailed the ewes slowly up to Mowich behind Horse Mountain to lamb part of the band, the others lambed around the Brown Ranch.

Fences were everywhere, no more open spaces. That was in April and the night we camped at the foot of Horse Mountain four inches of snow fell and ewes and lambs were kegged up in the storm. After two days and in time to save a real loss, the storm broke, the sun came out and little rivulets carried away the melting snow.

"As the sheep increased it seemed as though we just couldn't find space enough for them. From a simple little spread of Brown Ranch, Lava Beds, Mowich, Medicine Lake and Bulls Eyes, there came a time when I had sheep from the Bulls Eyes to Jenny Creek. We followed the snow line into Medicine Lake. We advanced as the snow retreated. I wonder how many people who quote "He leadeth me beside the still waters" have any conception of that line in the Shepherds Psalm."

The difficulties encountered by this amazing woman are hard to imagine in this time period. She reported: "What wild rides, over a burning bridge, through bogs and marshes, over high centers on Goodlow Mountain. Flat tires alone at midnight, hung up on a rock at 2 a.m. in the Devil's Garden beyond Bly. I remember driving one after-noon from the Jerry McCartie camp at Robinson Springs to Langell's Valley through brushy and marshy country over an almost invisible road with Lou Tuttle beside me on horseback, her lariat around her saddlehorn ready to give a pull if I bogged down."

Ida told me that while she acted as camp tender, the one thing that made the herders mad was for her to forget to bring "snoose" (Copenhagen).

While her father was still living, they bought the Hopkins Ranch on the north shore of Lower Klamath Lake. As time went on the depression of the 30's entered the economy of the livestock business. Ida wrote: "My sheep count had reached 8,000 head including the lamb crop. A man from Chico came up to receive the Brown half for the two widows. I hope they came out better than I did. $8.00 lambs were sold for $1.25, 50ç wool was a drug on the market at 25ç and 15ç. A good many years work went glimmering, but I certainly had lots of fellow sufferers." Ida and her father were unable to complete payment for the Hopkins Ranch so the Federal Land Bank foreclosed the mortgage.

Fortunately the O'Conners who later bought the ranch gave, at my request, the giant rock containing the many Modoc Indian bedrock mortars to the Klamath County Museum. They are now in front of the Museum labeled "Mortars Used by the Klamath Indians."

All the time the pressure of her economic activity was going on, Ida participated fully in the church, fraternal, patriotic and civic life of the community. She was the founder and first president of the Klamath County Historical Society. Having a sense of history at an ear-ly age, she gathered and preserved priceless perishable artifacts used

IDA MOMYER ODELL—Picture taken with a group at a party given in her honor by the Daughters of the American Revolution.

(Odell Collection)

by the Indians. These and other items were given to the Klamath County Museum.

One of her happiest events was her marriage in 1931 to Bob Odell, a gentle and cultured man. During the happy years of their marriage, he joined her in visiting many of the sentimental and historic places of their youth.

The Odells purchased an apartment in a retirement home in Salem. It was there that I called upon them when I was serving in the State Legislature. Ida and Bob were glad to see someone from Klamath County · even a politician. I was able to visit with them and to make some tape recordings but Ida was not satisfied with her ability to remember so allowed me to copy some of her memoirs. Later Bob Odell gave me much of their picture collection which will, with a few exceptions, end up in the Shaw Historical Library at O.I.T.

I was fortunate to be able to visit Ida several times. At the time of my last visit, Bob told me that the tiny woman was asleep and he did not wish to awaken her. From this sleep, she never awakened.

Like others in this book, I do not want this unusual person to be forgotten. Her feelings are best described by the eloquence of her own words:

"I have loved my Klamath more than anyone can ever know. Its vivid sunsets, its bare hills, and timbered mountains. Its vast lonely reaches, now a thing of the past. Lakes, springs and rivers. The smell of burning sagebrush, the taste of "sourdough" bread. It has been exciting, always interesting, but I would not want to live it over again. I am filled with gratitude for these later peaceful years, for financial security due to the wisdom of my beloved husband and most of all for him and his patience, kindness and love."

A GATEWAY TO THE SOUTH

From the time of the earliest travelers, going south and west from the Klamath Basin presented problems. The Cascades were a barrier on the west; the rivers and marshes on the south. Many of the marshy impediments have been removed by drainage and reclamation but, prior to 1909, developers and boosters of the region were frustrated by the lack of roads, especially railroads.

Freight from the south was picked up at the end of Klamath Lake Railroad (actually a logging road) at a place called Pokegama. Teams of from four to eight horses pulled the merchandise out of the deep Klamath Canyon, over the Topsy Grade and on to the Klamath River. Devere Helfrich said Keno was first used as a river port about 1872 and came into use as a passenger and freight transfer point from 1889 to 1903.

After 1907, three wagon routes converged at a place called Teeter's Landing, upriver from Keno and closer to the railroad terminal point. Passengers, as well as freight, were changed here to water transportation.

A description of the railroad, stage and water transportation was recorded by Sarah Welch Rightmier on the way to a homestead near Olene in 1906: "There are large rocks in the river and the water comes splashing against them, makes a beautiful scene. I only wish I had a Kodak. Here is an old fashioned rail fence. Now there are a few scattered pine trees. Here is a nice valley, to the right as we go up to Pokegama. It is in the shape of a horse shoe. It is beautiful scenery. Here we have a river and back up the mountains, it seems like. Now we go forward again. The Klamath River and valley is beautiful from this point. We are high up on the mountain switching back and forth, I don't know what is the matter, maybe a balky engine. Now we have on another carload of lumber and it was too heavy so they had to turn it loose, so we are sailing along at a pretty fast speed. The ground is covered with black irregular-shaped stones. I don't see any bunch grass to speak of. From the car the telephone line looks like a clothes line. It looks like I could reach it. We are at Pokegama. There are two stages ready to take us to Keno. One has six horses, the other had four horses. I rode in the stage that had four horses. I sit up on the seat with the driver. There are eleven people on our stage. We went to Keno and there took a steam boat and will go to the falls on the boat. It seems very nice and smooth, the lake is like a looking glass. It is 24 miles from Keno to Klamath Falls. I see quite a few water fowl of different kinds. Arrived at Klamath Falls, went to the Lake View Hotel, had a room in the third story. Will go over to Hot Springs this morning if I have time before I go to Olene."

"OLD BLUE"—The engine that pulled Mrs. Rightmier.   (Odell Collection)

Each time the railroad would be extended, the freight and stage routes would change. The new routes, in turn, would require new closer terminal facilities. Teeter's Landing was upriver and south of Keno. It had a hotel, dining room and a large warehouse in which merchandise moving from land to water could be stored. A long boat-landing dock fronted the warehouse.

Ambitious citizens in the bustling town, newly named Klamath Falls, could hardly wait until rail transportation would arrive. Among them was Abel Ady. He was interested in the development and sale of land, especially land in the region of Lower Klamath Lake. He felt that the passenger accommodations were not being properly managed and persuaded his wife Leona to manage the dining room. With Mrs. Ady was her small daughter Doris, now Mrs. Calvin Peyton. Doris said that they could look from their window toward the southeast and see when the stages or freighters came over the hill. This was a signal to get the food ready and the table set. Custom required linen tablecloths and napkins. These had to be laundered on a washboard, then ironed with stove-heated irons, a job to be remembered.

Having been properly trained in table manners, Doris looked with disgust at the wolfish-eating habits of the Ericksen-Peterson boat workers. On one occasion, she set the table with the kitchen ware rather than the proper table ware. Her mother discovered her revenge-move in time to change it to the proper cutlery.

84

Building a railroad that would support heavy locomotives across the marsh country presented formidable problems. A large dredge had to be provided and a suitable floating barge built upon which to mount the machinery. In order to build this, a sawmill had to be constructed to manufacture the barge and giant booms to hold the dredge. A portable sawmill was brought in and work progressed. Finally the clamshell dredge, the Klamath Queen, came into being.

The Southern Pacific Railroad was gradually pushing north from Montague; horses and men shoveling, blasting and pulling. By 1908, it had reached Grass Lake, California. From here, they hauled the cement for the construction of the Klamath irrigation tunnel. Horse freight teams delivered the cement to Laird's Landing on the southeast side of the Lower Klamath Lake. John McKay said that this terminal was a very busy place. The steamboat Canby was loaded at Laird's then went west into the Klamath River and on to Klamath Falls. Then teams delivered the cement to the north end of Link River where the construction took place.

Mr. McKay said that he was only a kid but he was given the job of hauling laborers from Grass Lake. John called them "hobos." He then scattered them out along the construction job sites. Young John was hired by the Marian-Reddick employment agency of Sacramento to pick new recruits up by the wagonload.

The railroad by-passed the old town of Picard and came through

BUILDING THE QUEEN—The large timbers required construction of a sawmill before the Queen could be built at Ady. Ady children watch workers assemble the giant dredge. (Peyton Collection)

STEAMBOAT TENDER—The railroad cars have reached the area near Furber Marsh but the Queen is still served by a steamboat tender.

(Peyton Collection)

GOING TOWARD MIDLAND—Removal of earth for the railroad grade left deep canals on either side. This simplified the movement of fuel and supplies by boat.

(Peyton Collection)

the area where the town of Dorris now exists. Most of the buildings from Picard were moved to the new townsite on the railroad by winch and horsepower. This move, though skillfully done, was very slow. I was told that as the grocery store was moved, they continued to serve their customers as the building was moved along.

North of the Dorris tunnel, a man named Woody operated a saloon. It was a real profitable venture but it closed after the railroad was constructed.

John McKay said a human life was worth very little in a railroad camp. He felt sure there were a number of bodies buried in the railroad earth fill north of Dorris.

As the Klamath Queen lifted great buckets of mud to form the railroad bed, Thomas McCormick, owner of the steamboat Canby, could see that his route through the Straits into Laird's Landing, Oklahoma Landing and to the Merrill area would soon be cut off by the new construction. He threatened to leave his boat, Canby, moored in the narrow straits where the rails would cross but he said that Jerry Martin at the bank had persuaded him that it would only impede progress.

Progress soon put an end to the lively river port at Teeter's Landing. The new terminal was named for the father of little Doris Ady. Docking facilities were built where steamboats could meet the train at the straits of the Lower Klamath channel. Meanwhile, the dredge pushed on toward Midland and it was here that Mr. Ady built a house. Extensive cattle corrals were built at Midland to provide a closer shipping point to serve the livestock industry moving animals to California markets.

By 1909 the Klamath Queen had conquered the soft, treacherous marshlands and the first train arrived in Klamath Falls. The band and the dignitaries were out to meet the new blessed event. That same day they were selling rides in a new contrivance called an automobile.

Upon reaching Klamath Falls, the work of the Queen was not over. There were more marshes and a long route along the west side of the lakebed before the virgin forests of northern Klamath County could be taken to market. Link River is only a mile long but it represents an impassable barrier to boat transportation.

Could the Queen be moved? Erickson-Peterson thought so. Timber fallers were sent to Ashland to bring back oak tree trunks. After drying, they were turned in a lathe in the shop of Harry Goeller to make rollers. The Queen was rolled out of the lake by horse power winches, then rolled up California Avenue to be refloated and a big new job undertaken. The oak rollers were kept and were later to be used to move the big wooden courthouse to Walnut Avenue where it became the Walnut Apartments. Assisting in the new construction on the Upper Lake was a newly built larger dredge, James O'Grady.

After the Southern Pacific job was finished to Barclay Springs, the Queen was purchased by E. P. McCornack for reclamation work at

NEW CROPS—Land that had been worth only $2 to $4 an acre could now produce crops for export. The new invention called the automobile illustrates the height of the new alfalfa crop.

Caledonia and Wocus Marsh. About 1927, a new barge was placed under the machinery then renamed the Cardinal.

It would not be long before the new gateway to the south would change the character of the Klamath region. The lands that had produced only pasture could now grow other crops for market. The former cow town would become a lumbering center. The income from sale of Klamath Reservation timber would change the economy and way of life of the Indians who owned it.

MERLE WEST AND THE WOBBLIES

A graduate of Cornell College in Iowa, Merle West came to the Klamath country in 1914 from Douglas County. He was one of the principal owners and managers of the Big Lakes Box Co. In addition to this, he was affiliated with the old American National Bank, West Hitchcock Company and International Truck Dealers. He shared ownership of the Allis Chalmers distribution center for tractors and construction equipment.

In 1915, Merle and Emma West purchased a farm in the Henley district that later became Rolling Hills subdivision. My acquaintance with Merle occurred after I bought my present home place from lawyer R.C. Grosbeck. Although neither of us lived on our farm property at the time, we called each other "neighbor" and joined in personally building a new fence to replace the badly deteriorated old one.

In our discussions, I learned that Merle had a remarkable memory and store of information. He could report the recent price of raw lead as well as the price of fir two by fours. He was both politically and economically literate.

Merle had retired and was living in the Winema Hotel when he called me to come to his office and said that he had a story to tell that should not be forgotten. He also asked that it not be released until after his death. I made a tape recording at that time of his story which follows in his own words:

"During the war period of World War I, a lot of the younger folks, of course, were in the service and it was rather difficult to get help especially up in this part of the country. They had an employment agency that the lumbermen themselves operated down here run by Jimmie Ryan, a timber cruiser, and they would ship men in from Portland, Sacramento and San Francisco to take these various jobs. They would have to pay them wages and guarantee them so much but no telling what kind of help you might get.

"During that time, the people in the farming country and all over this western country, as well as the timber, had a lot of trouble with sabotage. There were a lot of grainfields burned and haystacks burned and so on. Somebody in the area was just "raising ned." The lumbermen were having all kinds of trouble, more perhaps in the woods than any place else. They would fall the logs one over another so they would break them up. They would have a marker mark the length they were to be bucked and then they would be bucked a few inches short so instead of having a 16 foot log that would make 16 foot lumber, it would have to be trimmed back to 14 and all that sort of thing. They would drive railroad spikes into the logs, drive files into the logs and break them up. When the logs hit the mills it would wreck the saws and there was all kinds of sabotage that was going on in that way. They had fires going too at times and I don't know it seemed that the more you fought the fire the bigger it got and they found out that some of the firefighters themselves, by George, were keeping the fires set.

"Well, as far as the lumbermen themselves were concerned, they thought it would be advisable to try to find out who some of these fellows were and it was legal at that time to bring in a detective. It just so happened that Gus Krause and myself were elected as the committee to handle this detective stuff. We hired a man out of San Francisco and he came up and in a few weeks didn't seem to be getting anywhere so we sent him back and we hired another one. He might have been a little better but not very much so we sent him back but the third one we got really knew his stuff. A slight fellow in build, he appeared as an eccentric. He wore glasses. I don't know whether they had rims or not but he would go down the street with a paper up in front of his face and dodged from one side to the other and so on. People would say, "Why don't they kick that fellow out of town? He has no business here and he must be up to something." Well, he was up to something, by George, he hadn't been here too long until he became secretary of the IWW, the Wobblies, who were causing all this trouble. He did such a good job of it that he kept all their books and everything and he had members listed in the books and he had their addresses and so it was really kept up to snuff.

"Well, when Martin Brothers' mill was burned that was along in the middle of July. It was late one night that it happened, I think sometime after midnight at their mill and elevators that were down at the corner of Spring and 6th street. The fire department at that time was not too good and the result of the fire was that it was a total loss. There were embers flying all over the country. They had watchers at the Standard Oil Co. that was across the street. They had others watching around the yard and roofs of the Ewuana Box Co. and the Big Lakes Box Co. and while this fire was going on there were a number of fires that started that were put out before they got going and all because of these people stationed around just to do that very thing.

"The community, by the time the fire was out, was pretty well aroused to the situation and they assumed that the Wobblies had set the fire. George Humphrey, who was sheriff at that time, so naturally he was out so George wanted to cooperate but he didn't have enough deputies to handle the thing so he appointed a lot of the younger fellows in town as deputies. So the first thing they did was to raid the headquarters of the Wobblies. At that time, they had a building facing on 4th street right back of the present office of the power company. Well, when they raided that they found these books where they were available with all this information in it. So I don't know who it was, but anyway they called the guys in and they'd say, "Well, you two fellows go up to Pelican Bay's camp and in cabin so-and-so you'll find such-and-such guy. Bring him in." They did that until they covered all the lumber area. The other deputies that were appointed watched all the incoming and outgoing traffic whether it was on the railroad or any of the streets and roads around. They were patrolled 24 hours a day and nobody got in town or out of town without being known. In the mean-time, they brought these fellows in and took them down to the city hall. Joe Smith was chief of police at that time and Sam Walker was his only deputy. Well, anyway Sam frisked all these fellows when they came to see what they had on them and so on and threw them in jail. I guess they had the jail filled up so nobody could lie down. They just had to stand.

"Well, they chewed around among themselves and finally they sent a wire to a Portland attorney to come down to represent them. Well, of course, that wire was intercepted and they knew that the at-torney had wired back just when he would be here and how. So he finally got back and he got into town and what he did there was a bunch of the boys met him down at the depot and took him to the car in the street and went down Main Street to the Hall Hotel. He said, "Here's where I'm getting off." They said, "Yes, you are, you so-and-so." They took him on down to the other end of town and talked to him for awhile and he was rather belligerent but he finally came to the conclusion that they meant business as one of the boys said, "Where's that rope? Didn't you bring it down?" "Oh, he said, "I'll go get it. I forgot it but it's right up here." So he went and got a rope and threw it over the cross arm of a telephone pole and stretched this fellow's neck a little bit. He said, "You know you don't belong in Klamath County. There's a train leaves Ashland over here at such and such a time and we've got just about enough time to get over there to catch the train. But, of course, the fare will have to be paid in advance and there's one condition if we take you over there and that's if you never stick your nose in Klamath County again. Is that agreeable?" He said, "Yes sir, yes sir, I'm ready to go."

"Well, the federal authorities came in to look over these fellows that they had in jail and they took some of them that they had been looking for among the group and they took them out and they kept the rest of them in jail for awhile and gradually they turned this one loose and the other one loose with the understanding that they would keep out of Klamath County too and I don't suppose they have ever been back. I don't know but the detective, of course, was the one they were after first so he was the first one to be thrown in jail. Well, then they had to spill the beans and they told the sheriff who he was so he was taken out of the jail because he was 'too violent a man and too dangerous a man to have in the jail' so they put him in solitary confinement. Well, of course, that consisted of putting him on the first train out because his life wouldn't have been worth anything had he stayed around here."

The following article appeared in the Klamath Falls newspaper on Monday, July 16, 1917:

CITIZENS OF KLAMATH HAVE TAKEN STAND TO WIPE OUT MENACE RALLY TO PRESSING NEED OF THE COMMUNITY WITHOUT DELAY

"Large crowd of men offer services and are sworn-in as deputies to aid local officials in work of rounding up I.W.W. All suspicious characters are taken in. Roads to city guarded.

Paralyzed at first by the audacity of the fiends who burned the Martin Mill, men all over the city quickly awoke to the necessity of immediate and strenuous action to prevent the repetition of the imfamous deed by putting all those who were thought to be leagued with the I.W.W. movement where they would be secure for the time being, and by the middle of the forenoon nearly a hundred deputy sheriffs had been sworn in at the city hall, extra guards put at all the mills and factories and nearly all the roads were being patrolled for suspicious characters. Before noon several of the ringleaders of the I.W.W. were safely locked in the cells of the police station, and by the middle of the afternoon nearly thirty had been taken in.

"Not the slightest doubt appeared in the mind of anyone as to the source of the fire. A. Stiplen, a laborer of this city, who is well and favorably known declared before a group of officers and citizens in the mayor's office yesterday that he was approached about 9 o'clock to attend their meeting and that he accepted their invitation.

"Arrived there, he found only a few men, and evidence of a great deal of whiskey. He was asked to get "lined up" with the organization, and refused with the statement that he was too patriotic to join such a body in times like these. The members then voiced their surprise that an intelligent man such as he appeared to be, held patriotic sentiments, and affirmed that this was the time to strike, when there was a chance of a success.

"Stiplin declared further that there were German spies now at work in the box factories of the city."

"New I.W.W. suspects continued to be picked up by the different patrols around the city. Between thirty-five and forty are now being held. On twelve or fifteen the I.W.W. membership cards were found. The men have been picked up in all sections. With the membership list found at the headquarters yesterday to guide them, the officers and deputies are leaving no stone unturned to corral all who are believed to have any connection with the disturbers.

"John Finnell has been appointed United States Deputy Marshall and attorney J. H. Carnahan, United Sates Deputy Attorney by District Attorney Clarence Reames of Portland.

"Two secret service men who have been here for sometime were of great assistance to the sheriff.

"Among the correspondence secured yesterday at the raid made on I.W.W. headquarters were instructions for the local officers, to cache all papers etc., relating to the work of the organization, at some point outside the headquarters. This order had evidently not been complied with at the time of the raid."

Following the incident, Merle said:

"There was some sabotage went on afterwards but not a great deal. Practically all of it stopped. The Martin Brothers mill was the principal outlet for the grain that was grown here and most of the flour that was used in the area. A few of the farmers had some space to store their grain but most of it had to be shipped out as they weren't able to rebuild in time to take care of the crop.

"What were some of the major industrial plants at that time? Ackley Brothers Mill was down on Klamath Avenue and Center Street, one of the oldest in the community. Then there was the Ewauna Box Co. and the Big Lakes Box Co., right next to that. There was Klamath Lumber and Box in Shippington, the Pelican Bay Lumber Co. and Algoma Lumber Co. I think Lamm Lumber Co. had been built at that time too. Then there were several small mills built up near Chiloquin. At that time Blocklinger was at Dorris. It was before he had built his mill at Chiloquin. Then there were the Turner Brothers who had a mill out on Stukel Mountain. Worlow had a mill on Bryant Mountain. Most of that lumber was used by the farmers in building.

"The main lumber products that went out of here were used in boxes. As far as the total cut was concerned, it was practically all pine and the major portion of the pine was cut in the sizes for remanufacturing of boxes. The balance of the stock, which was largely shop type lumber, was shipped to the remanufacturing places in the middle west along the Mississippi River principally."

Merle West had a wide variety of interests. He encouraged Frank Payne, an employee of "Big Lakes", in his searches for Indian artifacts than later joined Andy Collier and Tom Watters in the purchase of his collection for the Winema Hotel. Merle was, of course, interested in community affairs including athletics.

It is fortunate for the Klamath country that Merle and his wife, Emma, were wise investors and "savers." Emma told us that they had a budget and she kept careful records of their family expenditures.

MERLE WEST—A "Gibraltar" of a man, Merle had a ready smile and a gentle voice. He had a high standard of achievement for himself and was able to convey his expectations to others. His broad knowledge led to success in many fields of endeavor.

(Earl Kent Photo)

They proved that savers can also be generous. Emma died several years before her husband. Her sizeable estate was given to the Shrine Hospital for Crippled Children.

In Merle's will, one million dollars was left to little Cornell College for a building. About $300,000 was willed to the Shrine Hospital and over a million dollars was given to the Presbyterian Intercommunity Hospital in Klamath Falls. They honored him by renaming it the Merle West Medical Center.

The West legacy to the future youth of the county was the greatest. It established a scholarship fund in excess of three million dollars called the Merle S. and Emma J. West Scholarship fund. This fund, to be administered by the U.S. National Bank, is estimated to bring in from two hundred to three hundred thousand dollars each year. This money is to be given to deserving scholars who want to attend college.

THE CITY OF CHILOQUIN IS BORN
THE GIENGERS

It was the first time the passenger had ridden the Southern Pacific train going north from Klamath Falls. He had traveled to the village at Chiloquin before but never on the train. He, of course, knew when the engine crossed the Klamath Reservation line at Barclay Springs. A short time later the train stopped. A shot rang out, then another!! He looked out to find the reason for the shooting when another more experienced passenger told him it was just the train conductor stopped to hunt ducks along the shore of the lake.

The passenger on this day was Albert Charles Gienger, a man whose energy, creativity and dedication would become a major force in the development and destiny of a former Indian Village called Chiloquin.

The town was given its name from the head man of the village who was called Chal-o-quin. Samuel Clark was apparently the only newspaper man to interview the old warrior. Clark, a New York Times reporter, spent some time with him in 1873 with the help of Chaloquin's son, Mose, as interpreter. Clark wrote that Chaloquin and his brother, Beaded Hat, formerly lived with their father, the chief of Ouxy on the Klamath Marsh. Chaloquin apparently moved to the forks of the Sprague and the Williamson after he became an adult. When the various village heads came together to sign the Treaty of 1864, he signed and the village took his name. It was probably unpronounceable for Caucasian tongues so it became Chiloquin.

The principal Indian population centers in pre-Columbian times were near the mouth of the Williamson River and on the Klamath Marsh. Establishment of Fort Klamath and the agencies at Yainax and Agency Creek had a tendency to move an already fairly mobile people to those centers. At the coming of the railroad, Chiloquin was a pretty small village occupied principally by Indians.

The actual allotment of individually owned land to the Indians began with the leadership of Jesse Lee Kirk. According to Stern, it took place about 1885.

The sale of timber on the allotted lands began in 1911 after the railroad came. The first sale of tribal timber occurred in 1913. Construction jobs, railroad jobs and other work soon brought Chiloquin a population exceeding the former centers. Albert Gienger, a grocery man in Klamath Falls, first bought a store in Chiloquin about 1913. There was no water system, electricity or municipal government. After this time, the Gienger family, while in and out of business there, was to have an impact on the village that continues to this day.

ALBERT CHARLES GIENGER, THE FOUNDER—Innovative and courageous, he was willing to take risks that at times proved discouraging. At other times, he enjoyed the glow of success.

After a period of farming near Sprague River at Kawamkan Springs, the Giengers opened a general merchandise store in Chiloquin. A well was drilled and people were allowed to hookup to the water line. As population grew, problems arose so Albert Gienger was elected justice of the peace. On one occasion an Indian was brought to him by the Indian Police charged with gambling. Actually prior to the interference of the white man, gambling had been the primary form of recreation for the Klamaths, as well as most other Indian tribes. The prisoner said he knew of another who had gambled so the second man was brought in. As the prisoners increased, the informants increased until in desperation the judge dismissed the charges against the lot of them.

On another occasion, the frontier justice was confronted with the problem of several convicted prisoners with no jail to put them in. Being a practical man, he had them incarcerated in a box car on the nearby Southern Pacific tracks. He later ordered them released before the next train arrived to haul the car away. (Shades of the A.C.L.U.)

If Chiloquin took advantage of the railroad, the railroad also exploited the city. At times, pullman cars of excursionists would be parked on a siding close to Williamson River near town for a week at a time so they could go fishing.

The Gienger well was finally declared contaminated so had to be abandoned. Then a water line and pump was extended to the river. This was a temporary solution. Streets and sewers also needed to be maintained. A municipal government was finally formed and "Dad" Gienger was elected as the first mayor.

Meanwhile, son LeRoy, known to everyone as Roy, had grown up working in the Grocery story in Klamath Falls, on the ranch at Kawamkan and now in the new store at Chiloquin. I asked him how they got along dealing with the Indians. He said, "Fine. At times there was a little feuding between families but generally everything was peaceful." On one occasion Roy became sick while he was living behind the store. Billy Moore, head of the Shaker Church, came to see him and asked if his people could help make him well. His answer was "Yes" so then they came with bells and while chanting prayers, they marched around his bed ringing the bells. I asked Roy if this made him feel better and he said it did.

Another Indian doctor that Roy knew well was Lee Snipe. Snipe was a real showman. He wore midwestern buckskin Indian clothing and a feather war bonnet. He carried a feather "coop stick" made from the end of a broken fish pole. He completed his outfit with deer-hoof rattles, a genuine Klamath tradition. He was quite active and quite influential in the healing arts.

One of the problems in managing a store at Chiloquin was the same as Momyer encountered at the Agency- that of extending credit. Most who ran charge accounts would pay. Some were so honest that, in addition to credit for groceries, money could be loaned to them with the assurance that they would pay it back. The worst problem was with Agency personnel. Indians learned that, as government wards, the creditor had no right to collect debts from their allotment received from timber sales. The creditor was simply told by Indian Service personnel that they should know better than to extend credit to an Indian.

It was not long after the coming of the railroad that Chiloquin became a place of great activity. In 1914 Wilfred Lamm established a sawmill at a place called "Lelu" later named Modoc Point. In 1916 a small mill was built on the Williamson River about one mile north of town. This was taken over about 1924 by Forest Lumber Company, which completely rebuilt it and greatly increased the capacity. In 1918 Blocklinger, who had operated at Dorris, built a large mill in town on the Sprague River. In 1919 Bedford and Crane started a mill on the same river east of town.

Jobs in the sawmills were only part of the economic impact. Branch logging lines were extended from Kirk to tap the virgin forests on tribal lands. As the trees were harvested, new rail lines were built. The contract laborers who built the lines were mostly Swedes, big, strong, hardworking and big spenders. They brought new wealth and activity and problems to Chiloquin.

A new brick store building had been built and was operated by son Roy but it was not all downhill for the Giengers. Competition was fierce, even in politics. R. C. Spink, owner of a competing store, ran for mayor against the senior Gienger. It was said in town that every Indian was voted twice and the drunk ones three times.

As mayor in the 1930's, an almost unheard of accomplishment was made. Dad Gienger, through persistence and skill, was able to persuade the U.S. Congress to allow Chiloquin to operate a city-owned tavern. Previously, it had been illegal to sell alcoholic beverages on an Indian reservation. The license enabled the city to accomplish many things with the revenue- with paving, sewers, etc. without levying excessive property taxes.

In the meantime, another Gienger entered the picture. Elvine Flury had come in 1921 to teach in Klamath County at the Horton School. This was in Poe Valley on the north side of Lost River. An unusual aspect of this teaching assignment was that many of the students were from Russian refugee families. She said that their habits were strange. The whole family ate from one kettle. Three of her students spoke no English but they were very musical and loved to dance. Apparently, she did well with them as one of the families gave her a live turkey under the school Christmas tree.

Elvine's sister, Josephine Wolff, and her husband, Henry, ran a bakery at Chiloquin. It was while working at the bakery that Elvine met

SCENE IN GIENGER STORE—About 1930 · In those days people were "waited on." (Note the pickle barrel.)

98

young Roy Gienger. This was a blessing for Chiloquin as she married him in 1926. She became an active member of the community, joining in fraternal and civic affairs. She developed an interest in the crafts and cultural traditions of the Klamaths. Over the years, the Indians brought baskets and other perishable items to give her and to sell to the store. These have been carefully catalogued and documented.

It was in the office of Dr. Luther S. Cressman at the University of Oregon, where I first met Mrs. Gienger. She was studying how to preserve and catalogue the precious items. I did not realize that about forty years later I would be studying the valuable catalogue in doing archaeological research for the U.S. District Court of Portland.

Meanwhile, in the dry windy 1930's, she and the family made trips to the Fort Rock Desert and recovered an unusual collection of the ancient pieces from the desert. This was at the time when government agencies had encouraged the Klamaths to forget the past and prepare for the future. School children were shown the collection but it has now been placed in storage for safe keeping. Future generations of both Indians and others will sometime be able to look at this wonderful heritage.

Mrs. LeRoy Gienger was appointed to the Klamath County Museum Commission when the museum was founded. Her contributions and advice were invaluable.

Destiny again played a part in my relationship with the Giengers in 1948 when Mr. Percy Dixon, chairman of the Klamath County School Board, called upon me at the State Department of Education where I was employed. He suggested that I meet with the board to apply for the position of district superintendent. It was here that I met school board member, Roy Gienger of Chiloquin. His quick intelligence and desire for action soon became apparent.

The district had accumulated building funds from a three-mill levy, enough to fund the building of the Peterson School. The population increase in the suburban and Henley area was so rapid that this construction would absorb only a small part of the needs. What to do? The board did not want to incur bonded indebtedness. Mr. Gienger proposed a ten-mill levy, enough to build a school each year. I swallowed hard. He said, "Times are good now. People can afford to pay taxes." I asked if they wanted to appoint a building advisory committee to help in promoting the levy. Roy's reply, "We are the advisory committee. That's why people elected us." The board agreed with Gienger and a new school project was completed each year debt-free.

When I assumed the school job, the district had already made overtures to state and federal authorities to get a reasonable financial contribution for the vast non-taxable federal holdings on the Klamath Reservation. A bill was passed in Congress allowing Indians to make a

ELVINE AND LEROY GIENGER IN 1945—Elvine and Roy Gienger have been in-separable since their marriage. They were active in community affairs when they were in business. Since retirement, the Giengers have traveled over the world. Much of their time has been spent studying the Indian cultures of Mexico and the Southwest.

payment each year from tribal funds. Indians are not dumb. How would you like to be "allowed" rather than "required" to pay income taxes? Since I did not want to be laughed out of the meeting, I did not even try to meet with the Tribal Council. I did discuss the problem with Seldon Kirk, tribal leader, who was courteous but noncommittal.

About this time Forrest Cooper sent me a federal appropriation bill that applied to the Hupa Reservation in California. As a long shot, I drafted a similar bill allocating only those portions of the cost that might be applied to students arising from non-taxable property. Sam Coon introduced the measure and with the help of Senator Guy Cordon a 65% appropriation was made for a new grade school at Chiloquin. The old Blocklinger mill site was acquired. School children were invited to make Indian designs for decorating tile on the school's exterior. Morrison and Howard Architects supervised the making of the ceramic plaques and the school was so unique it was published in the American School Board Journal. Normally there is some trouble from vandalism around a building site. In this case, the Chiloquin kids were so proud of their new school that there was no damage or problems. Funny thing- the Indian Service sent a man from Albuquerque, New Mexico, each month to be sure that we were actually building a school.

Economists tell us that a thing has value only if someone wants it.

Hall Scene in Chiloquin Grade School

As the railroads permitted the lumberman to have access to reservation timber, the value increased. By 1955, most of the sawmills in the Chiloquin area had closed. Large operators in Klamath Falls still bid on reservation timber but there were many small tracts that were held in the estates of those who had owned allotments. Some of these estates were held by 8 to 16, even 32 heirs. As wards of the U.S. Government, the development of the land or sale of timber became difficult if not impossible. Finally, government approval came for the sale of these estates to the highest bidder.

Merchant, cattleman, farmer Roy Gienger became logger Gienger. He bid on small estates giving value to property that had been frozen. Logs were sold to whomever would buy them. Don Magee of the Bly Sawmill said he had purchased lots of logs from Gienger without any written contract and that they had never had a disagreement or an argument.

Gienger's Store had become Gienger Enterprises. A third and fourth generation now live and work in the Chiloquin area. A small sawmill and pole factory at Lelu (Modoc Point) has provided employment in spite of weak lumber prices when other mills were closed. Fiercely loyal to the little city at the forks of the river, they and their marriage partners have become teachers, church workers, store managers and loggers. Strong family ties extend over many miles to even a fifth generation. Regardless of any of its faults or cultural disadvantages, they all know that Chiloquin is still the land of opportunity and the capital of the Gienger clan.

THE PEACEMAKER
Dibbon Cook

It would be hard to find a more peaceful and beautiful setting than the property where the Klamath Indian Agency was placed. Tall, stately old-growth pine trees were underlain by the well watered grass. The grounds around the white, wooden Agency building were carefully tended.

I had been invited to the agency to sit in a Tribal Council meeting as a representative of the Klamath County School District.

The ruling body of the tribe, called the Executive Committee, had difficulty in getting enough members to attend in order to have a quorum to legally transact business under their constitution. In order to encourage attendance, transportation had been provided to members living at a distance on the reservation. A free dinner was also provided.

As members drifted into the meeting, greetings were exchanged. Some were old and crippled and others came and brought children. I knew a few members but not many. One young man offered to sell me a large twelve pound trout. I explained that while it was legal for him to sell fish, it was not legal for me to buy it.

Inside the meeting hall, the scene was anything but peaceful and serene. The tribal rolls included three different groups of Indians who had in prehistoric times occupied different geographical territories; the Klamaths to the north, Modocs of the south and eastern territory and the Yahooskin band of Snakes, who had lived on the Sprague and Sycan Rivers near Beatty.

As the meeting progressed, it was evident that a great conflict existed among the various groups. Strong language (no profanity) and accusations were made during the debate. The meeting was presided over by Seldon Kirk, Chairman of the Tribal Executive Committee. He was a man of great dignity and poise. It was obvious in the rough and tumble of the acrimonious debate that all participants had respect for Mr. Kirk. Some of the speakers were much like the Indian orators of more primitive times. Unhurried and unruffled by their antagonists each pursued arguments to the end. Under the parliamentary rules, the older Indians would sometimes ask that the debate be translated into the Paiute language or the Klamath, which the Modocs also understood.

At a table with books and a tape recorder sat an Indian man who was the picture of tranquility. He had an almost continuous pleasant smile for any and all of the participants. This man was Dibbon Cook, Secretary of the Executive Committee.

Strangely enough, the divisions and conflicts of the group were not based upon tribal ancestry nor the geographical location of their residences on the reservation. Dibbon said that some feeling of status difference existed based upon the degree of Indian blood. Full bloods did not feel those of one-fourth Indian blood should have the same status. Voting rights, of course, were extended to any on the tribal rolls. At the time of my visit to the Agency, the main issue related to termination of federal supervision over the reservation. What was the background of the man who seemed to have the confidence and friendship of all factions?

Dibbon Cook was born at Pokegama near the California border. His father was George Cook, a Shasta Indian; his mother, Amelia Skeen, a Modoc. Shortly after his birth they moved to Shovel Creek where his father worked at the Klamath Hot Springs Resort. Young Dibbon soon discovered that there was money in the tourist business. The Klamath River Canyon had and still has an abundance of rattlesnakes. Dibbon's little dog could locate the snakes and Dibbon would then kill and skin them. Visitors at the resort would pay one dollar for a dried rattlesnake skin with the rattles attached. Young Dibbon said that his dog knew how to deal with snakes and neither he nor his dog was ever bitten. Of course, he explained, that he could never pull them from the rocks by their tails or he probably would have been bitten.

Following the death of his mother when he was only three years old, relatives came to move him by team and wagon over the Topsy

REMAINS OF OLD RESORT—A popular place that could be reached by Eastern tourists. George Cook worked here at the time son Dibbon was born.

Grade to live with an aunt at the Agency headquarters at Yainax. Here he attended a U.S. Government school called Day School No.1. Day School No.2 was at Beatty and Day School No.3 was located at Paiute Camp north of Beatty.

The school at Yainax only had four grades. Dibbon said that after passing the fourth grade, he spent four more years in that grade where he pretty well memorized the curriculum.

The U.S. Boarding School was located at the Klamath Agency where his next educational experience took place. Enrolling as a fourth grader, he said that they soon put him in the sixth grade but he applied to attend the Indian School at Riverside, California. At Riverside they refused to let Dibbon rest in the fourth grade and moved him to the seventh. he graduated in 1917, then went to Haskell Institute where he became proficient in shoe and harness work.

Soon after Haskell, Cook was offered a teaching job in the school at Fort Bidwell. His understanding of Indian psychology and tradition proved to be a great asset in his new work.

Dibbon said that the Paiute boys at Fort Bidwell were rather bashful and it was hard for him to communicate with them. "I went and bought fifty cents worth of candy. In those days, fifty cents would buy a whole sack of candy. There were about thirty boys and I told them that if they could take me down that I would give them the candy. It wasn't long before they took me down but after that I got along well with them."

When Cook returned to Yainax, a new sawmill had been built and a new town called Sprague River was established. After helping Dave Skeen move the Wolford and Wann Store from the Agency property to the new town, he went into the leather working business. In 1940 he was married to Esther Sargent of Chiloquin. They moved into a

SUB-AGENCY SCHOOL AT YAINAX—This picture taken about 1890 was before the town of Sprague River was founded.

home not far from the building he had helped to move from Yainax.

At a time when internal conflict had undermined confidence in some of the tribal leaders, Cook retained the trust and friendship of most Indians. He refused to take a federal job with the Indian Service as he wanted to be independent of any pressure from them. He was elected as tribal secretary in 1945. He also served on the Welfare Committee where he encouraged able-bodied persons to find jobs in private employment.

INDIAN BOY'S BAND—Apparently military type uniforms were the rule when this picture was taken about 1902. The band was directed by Harry Momyer.

(Odell Collection)

INDIAN GIRL STUDENTS—These nicely dressed girls were boarding students at the Klamath Agency about 1902.

(Odell Collection)

DIBBON COOK WITH THE AUTHOR—This photo was taken in front of the Favell Museum after a meeting of the Museum Advisory Board.

During the turbulent period of withdrawal of federal supervision, he was a staunch friend and right-hand man for Seldon Kirk. His job on the Enrollment Committee was to determine who were enrolled members and eligible to receive the benefits at the time of termination. I suggested that it must have been a difficult and trying job. He said, "It was not a hard job because the rolls were to include those born before August 15, 1954. The committee had no authority to change that."

At the time that eligible tribal members were to decide whether to take their assets and withdraw, he said that 473 members decided to remain and 1660 chose to withdraw. Dibbon then became chairman of the remaining members.

In serving his people, Dibbon always took pride in his Indian ancestry. Like many tribal members, he was critical of Indian police methods. His heritage did not prevent him from participating fully with non Indians in public affairs and private friendships.

Dibbon became well known as the honorary mayor of Sprague River. Officially he was on the school committee at that town and later in Chiloquin. Other service included Klamath County Bicentennial Committee, Advisory board of the Favell Museum, secretary of the Chiloquin Masonic Lodge of six years, master of the lodge in 1974. His late wife, Esther, was an active Republican and made a ceremonial gift of wocus to Mrs. Richard Nixon. Later Mrs. Cook became chairman of the County Republican Women.

Although more than eighty years old, Dibbon has not lost his interest in the tourist business. Now he manufactures arrowhead orna-

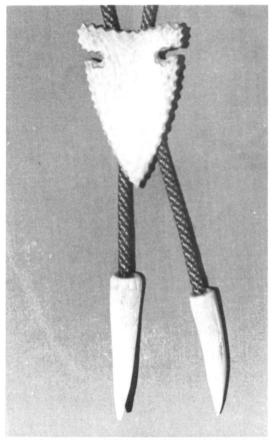

DEER ANTLER ORNAMENT—This bolo tie is an example of the skilled work done by Mr. Cook. Sale of these was stopped for a time by the Wildlife Commission.

ments and little animals from deer antlers by shaping them skillfully with leather working machinery. His work has attracted attention, especially from the Oregon Wildlife Commission who stopped sale of his products because it violated their rules. Representative Bob Kennedy introduced a bill to allow him to continue his handicraft and finally at a hearing in Salem the officials were convinced that deer shed their antlers each year so it was unnecessary to kill them in order to produce a bolo tie.

This unusual man is back in business each day proving that Indians can successfully compete and participate in the culture of the 20th century.

LIFE IN A LOGGING CAMP

At noon we always sat down in the shade to eat our sack lunch. Our boss, Clint Moore, usually took a short nap before getting us back to work. I looked down to see a small brown, spider-looking bug crawling on my caulked boot. Reaching for my saw oil, I applied a few drops, then the bug fell off. As a greenhorn in the Klamath country, I did not know an eastern Oregon tick when it crawled on me. There was a lot more I did not know about the pine woods but I was learning fast.

This took place at Weyerhaeuser Camp 2, the first large logging camp opened to supply the new pine mill. It is the largest in the world and located on the Klamath River west of Klamath Falls. I had worked in sawmills and at logging in the Willamette Valley, even learning to fire and punch (operate) a small donkey engine but here everything was different. There were no trucks or donkeys. Everything was railroad logging.

My crew on this day, known as Clint Moore's crew, consisted of 5 men and the boss. We were different from most Weyerhaeuser work gangs. Ronald Angus, a young man from Scotland, and Lloyd Frey were regular woods workers, the other three of us were college kids recruited to play baseball. We were all younger than most loggers.

BULLS WITH WAGON—The water powered McCormick Mill at Keno used logs pulled on wooden wheeled wagons with bulls. Lyle McCormick said the bulls were very gentle.

(Odell Collection)

Our assignment was to do anything we were told. On this job we were each given a water bag, a crosscut saw, mauls, wedges and saw oil. The saw oil was to be applied to the hand-operated cross-cut saws when pitch caused friction on the blade. In 1930 motor driven drag saws had been invented but these were useful only in fixed positions where little movement was required. The chainsaw would come much later.

The trees we were to cut into log lengths had been fallen earlier by a right-of-way crew who were clearing a path for the railway toward the west. The fallers who had preceded us evidently paid little attention to the position of the trees as they were in all directions and often pinched as we were bucking (sawing) them.

It was not easy to find a steady job in 1930. We were fortunate that the woods boss, engineer, Lloyd Crosby, was a baseball fan and that Monroe "Monty" Moore's father, Clint, was willing to tolerate young greenhorns on his crew. Monty played second base on our Camp 2 team. Vince Barrett was shortstop. Both had recently played at Southern Oregon. On first base was big Lou Veris out of the University of Montana. The pitcher was Leroy Huntley who had pitched for St. Ignatius in California (later San Francisco University). In the outfield were two Harvard guys and Al McCartney, son of the Weyerhaeuser general manager Ralph McCartney. The outfielders worked for Hal Ogle's crew which did fire control work and cut bug trees and snags. Our catcher, Milt Bias, had played a little professional baseball.

Our acceptance in the camp by the hard-boiled old professionals was much better than had we not been on the baseball team. After a few games, we often had many observers at our evening workouts. Also word was passed around that it might be profitable to bet on us.

Like the academic community and the military, logging camps have their "pecking order" and social status structure. The camp push was Sid Cruikshank who was over operations. Sid, Uppington and others in this category were called "Brass (obscenity)" and not even considered a part of the camp social structure. At the top of the working men's social order were the timber fallers called "Gypos" because they were paid according to their production. I recall that the railroad engineers and firemen looked to me like royalty. "Cat Doctors," tractor mechanics held a high status and the "Top Loader" who directed placement of the logs on the railroad cars was held in esteem. The "Hookers," who put hooks in the ends of the logs for loading, were below the "Boss Loaders." The jammer boss was almost in the "brass" category.

We had three "Powder Monkeys" who drove their own pickup. Their job was to go out on the right-of-way and find any rock im-

In Railroad logging when the trees around a railroad siding were removed, a new siding was built and loading equipment moved.

(Gene Gjertsen Photo)

The McGiffert loader at camp 2 could lift its flanged railroad wheels, then lower its legs so that the flatcars could pass underneath. Men placed the hooks at each end of the logs. This machine can now be seen in Collier State Park.

(Gene Gjertsen Photo)

pediments, then bore holes with a sledge hammer and star drill to blast away the rocks with powder. These men were treated with respect because we felt that they would get to heaven before us. "Cat Skinners" who dragged the logs to the railroad siding were people of stature. "Choker Setters" were somewhat lower on the scale.

In the field of education, if an unusually successful coach or teacher began to get independent and picky about the affairs of the building, they were sometimes called prima donnas. In logging when someone, usually a highly skilled individual, would become critical of the boss, the food, or working conditions and mentioned "going down the road," his fellow workers would say, "He's got the wrinkles off his gut."

In this camp many of the workers were involved in railroad construction. One segment of the work of Clint's crew consisted of building a railroad bridge across Spencer Creek. We took pride in this job but sometimes we were called upon to work with what was called the steel gang, a job with much sweat and little dignity. The boss was Steve Geneff, a former Bulgarian army officer. When he aroused his crew to work after lunch, I'm sure he could be heard halfway to Keno. Many of the steel gang had been with Weyerhaeuser in Washington and were transferred down. They represented many nationalities: Greeks, Romanians, one Russian, Turks- everything except Swedes and Norwegians.

One little man we called "Bolsheviki" attracted some attention for his courage. He would always stop work when any boss would approach him and stand and look the boss in the face. He would then resume his work when the foreman had passed on. We could not understand why he wasn't fired.

This steel crew was served by a locomotive called a shay. It had a boiler offset on one side with gears on the other. It was designed to work in steep grades but was slower than other railroad engines. The shay was accompanied by a flatcar load of rails and one of ties. A machine powered with steam from the locomotive would lift rails and ties from the cars, carry them in front to the crew, who then carried them in place where they were spiked down. The ties were not so bad to carry but the rails could get real heavy about quitting time.

The greatest injury to our dignity would come when we were required to work on the section gang called "Gandy Dancers." This work required pushing the cinder and gravel ballast under the ties along the track to level and straighten the rails. I always felt it was an insult to my caulked logging boots to use them in this work. The boss of the section gang was John Micheloff, a real gentleman of Greek descent. He had a college major in psychology. In social status, we considered section work lower than a whale's belly.

VIRGIN TIMER—A trainload of beautiful logs. No plywood manufacturing was done here in the early 30's.

The Weyerhaeuser Timber Company Camp 2 was a lot better place to live and work than most camps of that time. The bunkhouses were new and well made. Four men lived in each unit which had good beds and a stove. A man called the "Bull Cook" split the wood and carried it to each unit. In cold weather he built the fires. Another man called the "Game Warden" made the beds and I assume killed any insects, arachnids or mice found in the blankets. The bull cook and game warden had to be men of character lest they be tempted to sample the moonshine whiskey which loggers sometimes kept under their beds for medicinal purposes.

A sizeable shower house was available and those who lived in the married men's housing were permitted to use it. Married housing usually had two bedrooms, a living room and a kitchen. Each had an outside toilet of their own.

A company store or commissary carried most of the needs for groceries, gloves, soap, etc. Money was not needed, as script or coupons could be obtained from the company.

The cook house was something to behold. It was spotlessly clean. Each man had his favorite place at the table and woe be to anyone trying to usurp the turf of another. The food was great with two or three kinds of meat, pies, cakes, doughnuts and rolls always available. I have to believe the company lost money on the cook house as the hungry crews ate their fill.

The work assignments, whether logging or railroad, usually took us several miles into the woods. We were allowed travel one way on

"Cat Skinners" pulled the logs alongside the loader. By this time the big wheels had been replaced by the Aphey logging arch. This tracked log puller was less damaging to the forest floor and safer.

(Gene Gjertsen Photo)

company time. A gasoline-powered rail vehicle called a speeder pulled one or sometimes two crew cars to the work place. We were furnished with our own water bags which we could exchange when they became worn. A camp saw filer kept our saws sharp.

On Wednesday afternoons baseball players were sometimes brought in early to practice.

A portable public school was located on a railroad spur at the camp. For three years Beulah Elliott taught the lower six grades at camp while husband George bused the upper grades and taught at Keno.

Weyerhaeuser Camp was certainly better than other timber camps of the period. Ronald Angus, one of my work mates, said he nearly froze at a Pelican Bay Lumber Camp. "You could throw a cat through the cracks in the wall," according to Angus.

Public schools were maintained at Forest Lumber Company and Lamm's Camp in northern Klamath County. While doing summer work in 1932 for the school district, along with another teacher, I was assigned to go out, clean up the schools, varnish floors and get everything ready for the new year. We slept and ate at Forest Camp. I was amazed at the difference in the crews from the Camp 2 personnel. Here, if you couldn't speak Swedish or Norwegian, you could become very lonely. Most of these men were gypos who worked twice as hard and earned twice as much as hourly paid workers. Norse descendants did much of the lumber piling on a contract basis at the sawmills of Klamath County at this time too.

In Lake County there was a sawmill and camp near Drew's Valley called the Peterson Johnson Camp. The buildings were mostly made of board and bat rough lumber shacks. Jim DeVore, who lived there as a youngster, said one of the outstanding events he remembered was an occasional visit by a young man named Dick Reeder who brought clothing and shoes in a traveling van and displayed them for the residents of the camp. Loggers were fussy about their shoes and most of them wore good hats.

At Camp 2, I noticed that the men did not wear red wool underwear like the timbermen of the Willamette Valley region. I asked Dick Reeder about this and he said black underwear was the rule and he didn't even carry red. The black would, of course, last longer between washings.

The story was told to me of two Swedes at Peterson Johnson Camp who shared quarters with an Irishman. It was his custom to keep a bottle of whiskey hidden under his mattress. While the Irish lumberjack was in town, the Norsemen, in their loneliness, decided to share their good friend's illegal alcoholic stimulant and refill the bottle with tea.

Lakeview has long been a town where good Irishmen gather to reminisce and share their fellowship. After a long evening in Lakeview on Saturday night, our bunkmate from Peterson Johnson awoke with a bad headache and an awful thirst. With trembling hands, he reached for the bottle that would soothe his headache and quiet his nerves. Finding it in place, he hurriedly filled his mouth. Jumping from his bed, the enraged victim found his roommates gone. He rushed from his cabin to confront a neighbor. Raising his hands toward the heavens, he eloquently shouted: "May the harps of Erin never want for a string as long as there is a gut left in a G__ D__ Swede."

THE LOGGERS
Written for a plaque
at Cap Collier's Museum

Oh Stranger, ponder well what breed of men were these,
These Cruisers, Fallers, Skinners, horse and "cat,"
Chokesetters and the rest who used these tools.
No summer's searing dust could parch their souls,
Nor bitter breath of winter chill their hearts.
T'was never said they worked for pay alone,
Though it was good and always freely spent.
Tough jobs to lick they welcomed with each day,
"We'll bury that old mill in logs," their boast.
Such men as they have made this country great
Beyond the grasp of lesser breeds.
Pray God, Oh Stranger, others yet be born
Worthy as they to wear a Logger's boots!

(From Nelson Reed's book **Tule Smoke**)

FRED PETERSON
FATHER OF THE KLAMATH
COUNTY UNIT SCHOOL DISTRICT

When you finished school in the middle of the year, it was hard to find a teaching vacancy because contracts were for a full school year.

The young teacher at Southern Oregon Normal was pleased to be informed of a job in Klamath County. The year was 1927 and the oversupply of teachers made for great competition. After she received the contract, an appointment was made to meet the superintendent of the district who would take her to the new job at a school called Topsy.

Meeting her at the hotel, was a very large, round-faced man with a crew cut. Her suitcases were loaded into his car and they drove off in a westerly direction. Crossing the river at Keno, they continued finally turning off the Ashland highway before crossing the river again.

In the meantime, the superintendent was very affable and talkative. His continued conversation made it impossible for the new teacher to inquire about the conditions at the school or the location.

Soon the car, traveling on the narrow dirt road, left the mountain and started down into a deep canyon. She began to wonder why the previous teacher had resigned at mid-year. She wondered even more if they could travel safely down the winding road without an accident.

The deep canyon of the Klamath River provided a rough but passable trade route for the Modoc and Shasta Indians. The Columbia, the Klamath, and Pit River are the only rivers to cut through the Cascade Range.

There seemed to be no other vehicles traveling this day. The one-way conversation continued until they finally came to a residence in the bottom of the deep Klamath Canyon where the swift river cuts through the Cascade Mountains on the way to the sea.

The superintendent stepped out and knocked on the door but there was no answer. He turned and without hesitation took her suitcases inside. Then he went outside again where he rang the farm bell. The teacher was told to make herself at home as this was her boarding place. He left immediately without waiting for the return of the residents of the house in the deep canyon.

She looked around the house and it looked comfortable. On the walls were the mounted heads of animals and, of all things-photographs of Indians. It is not hard to imagine the anxiety of the young woman, whose popularity led to her election as the Queen of the May at Springfield High School, to find herself at the bottom of the Klamath Canyon in a house probably inhabited by Indians.

The teacher was Audrey McPherson, who later finished a highly successful career as girl's counselor at the Fremont Junior High School in Klamath Falls. The superintendent was Fred Peterson, who was not about to give the new teacher a chance to change her mind about teaching at Topsy.

The story had a happy ending. The people who occupied the house were the Frain family. Audrey found them delightful to live with and the small school a good place to teach the seven students. Wren Frain was son of Mart Frain, an early day Indian trader, and his mother, a member of the Shasta tribe. Mrs. Frain, Gussie, had been a longtime resident of the canyon region.

Prior to the coming of the railroad to Klamath Falls, the steep, winding roadway into the canyon was, and still is, called the Topsy Grade. It was a busy place traveled by both stagecoaches and freight carriers. The narrow curves made it a popular place for stagecoach robbers but now traffic was by automobile and very little of that. Audrey said that sometimes on Saturdays they would go to town (Klamath Falls) in Mr. Frain's Buick. He would take an iron crowbar and sticks of dynamite blasting powder. If the rocks which had fallen on the roadway were small enough, they could be pried off the road with the bar. If they were too large, one-half stick of dynamite expertly placed would send the boulder hurtling down the steep mountainside.

Mail for the small populace was delivered to a California post office, Beswick, six miles downriver from the Topsy School.

At the time Fred Peterson delivered Audrey McPherson to the Topsy School, the county unit system had been in operation only five years. It had passed through the first critical period where there was danger of dissolution but his determination to make the system work,

117

WINTER SCENE AT THE TOPSY SCHOOL IN 1927—The high fence was to keep the cattle out · not the children in.

that he had advocated and engineered, was motivation do do whatever was necessary.

Prior to the adoption of the county unit system of school organization in 1922, the disparity between the school districts was greater than almost any in the state. There were forty-two grade school districts outside the city of Klamath Falls, most maintained one-room schools. The district lines were often arbitrary with little relationship to population or assessed value. In 1920 the millage levy at Chiloquin was more than three times that of Crystal across the lake and twice that of Fort Klamath. Malin's levy was more than twice that of Bonanza. Shasta View school district near Malin had a levy thirty-three times that of Pine Grove near Henley.

The disparity between the quality of education, while not as great as the wealth, was unsatisfactory. Each district was governed by an independent board. The county superintendent (at that time, Twyla Ferguson) had little authority except to keep records.

Peterson's work as head of schools at both Bonanza and Merrill convinced him that the cure for these problems was adoption of the county unit organization. The Grange, an influential rural organization, opposed this movement but support at public meetings was offered by R. C. Groesbeck, an able and effective lawyer. After a heated campaign, the county unit system passed the vote on May 1922 of all county voters although the city school district number one was excluded as a first class district. The Klamath County Unit then became the largest district in the state.

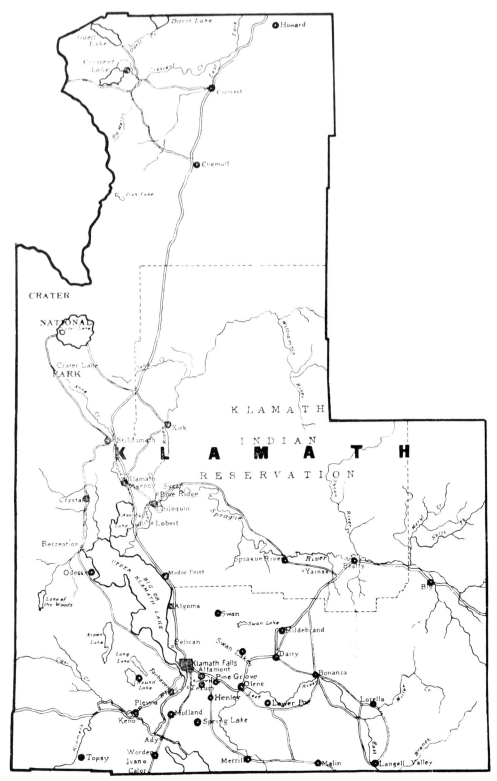

KLAMATH COUNTY SCHOOLS IN 1930—Although many small schools had been closed, there were still some operating in 1930. Five logging camp schools are not shown on this map.

119

Did the grateful parents and taxpayers congratulate Fred Peterson? Far from it! He told me that life was so rough he left town and went to live in Ashland for awhile until people cooled off. The county board of five appointed him clerk, then when the term of the elected county superintendent expired, he was made superintendent of the new district. A uniform elementary district levy of 3.8 mills was made to replace one that had been as high as 33 mills in one district.

The transition and acceptance of the new plan by the public came painfully and slowly. A music supervisor, Elizabeth Henderson, and an elementary supervisor, Isabelle Brixner was employed to improve instruction. Many supplies (except text-books) were furnished to pupils to equalize opportunity for poor children. A transportation system and repair shop was establish-ed. This made possible a reduction in the number of one room schools. The reduction was often met with hostility as some patrons wanted to keep their little school in their community. Sometimes a bus route would be established to run past a school, then the parents would eventually opt to send them to a multi-room program. The maintenance and sanitary facilities were greatly upgraded and janitor education programs developed.

Regardless of this great improvement in instruction and tax equity, pockets of opposition prevailed. The superintendent at teacher's meetings never failed to appeal for loyalty to the district and to each other. The county school board members wisely acted as a policy-making body and left the district ad-ministration to the superintendent. There was never any doubt that "Pete" (No one ever called him that to his face.) was the boss.

He zealously pursued this dedication to the public good, sometimes beyond the call of duty. On one occasion, he found a man had defrauded the district with a false transportation claim. An argu-ment arose and the man challenged him to a fight. They got in Fred's car and rode out to the Pine Grove school ground, then proceeded to engage in a fist fight. When the advantage seemed to turn to the schoolman's favor, the antagonist pulled a knife. Peterson, a powerful man, said that he then grabbed him and took the knife away and brought him back to town.

In some ways, Peterson was a strange combination. He was tough with a dollar. He had no use for alibis and was intolerant of anyone who was tardy. He inspected teacher's quarters when they lived in district-owned houses and made it known that he expected good house-keeping. Anyone who lacked a sense of humility could depend

120

upon him to help develop one. Yet, he would never seem to dismiss or fire anyone. He would sometimes chastise a person privately, then vigorously defend him publicly.

In the year 1936, the high school districts of the county opted to vote into the county unit district. This caused minor difficulties but the system had been so well-established and administered that only minor grumblings resulted. No admirer of previous high school administration, Peterson encouraged some grade school administrators: Glen Hale, Loy Barker, George Elliott and me, among others, to prepare for high school administration. We were always encouraged and often demanded to work in the public interest even if it meant self-sacrifice. None of us doubted his sincerity in this public dedication.

Peterson always favored a retirement system for teachers and felt that they should retire at age 65. He followed his own advice and retired from the superintendency in 1946. I later became superintendent and wondered how Fred would react to my extravagant and wild methods of school administration. He would often stop in my office for a visit but never offered suggestions on school administration. When people asked him about schools, he always feigned ignorance although I'm sure he had on many occasions defended me. Politically we almost always agreed and over the years he had indoctrinated me with the "public interest" compulsion.

What manner of background did this tough Swede have to enable him to build such an organization? His daughter, Maxine Sweetman of Portland, was kind enough to supply information of his family life that was previously unknown to me:

"My father was born in Galesburg, Illinois, in 1881 of Swedish immigrant parents. He had a challenging childhood: his mother died when he was 3, his step-mother when he was 6. The children were separated with the three girls living with an aunt and uncle and the three boys living with an alcoholic father. My father's schooling was minimal with the Lutheran minister insisting on some church school each year but there was no regular public school attendance. He tried going to college in Illinois but found it difficult to support himself at the same time. So he went to California, then headed for Oregon. When he got to Klamath Falls (1905) his pockets were empty, but a local hotel (The Hall, I think) allowed him to stay there; he found work and stayed the rest of his life."

Fred Peterson had very little college education. He told me he had attended a normal school for six weeks in Illinois and Maxine said that he had attended the Ashland Normal for a short time. Despite this lack of formal education, he was exceptionally well-informed. He used good English and was very perceptive of good teaching. Economical in the use of words, he expected others to be likewise. With this

FRED PETERSON—His crew-cut could be seen from Topsy to Gilchrist and Bly but was seldom photographed.

(Picture courtesy of Maxine Peterson Sweetman)

background, he was often suspicious of college professors, especially so when they rated an educational system on the amount of money spent per pupil.

In this age of advanced college degrees, Peterson would never be allowed to teach, let alone administer schools. Certificates were then issued upon examination in the various school subjects. Perhaps his greatest weakness was failure to foresee the great population growth in suburban Klamath Falls.

A vigorous and active man, Peterson operated a small dairy farm during most of the years he served as school superintendent. He usually had one hired man to do the work. He was married to a beautiful and gracious lady of a pioneer family, Nett Drew. They had two sons, Hal and Fred; one daughter, Maxine.

In retirement, Fred Peterson continued to be active in public affairs. He assisted in Grange work and was appointed to the County Welfare Commission. In those days, 25% of the welfare costs were borne by the county. They, in turn, had considerable authority in the administration of the program. Recipients were permitted to meet with the County Welfare Committee to present their case over the head of the social workers and head of the Welfare Administration.

One man from the Bonanza area had met with the Committee to complain. Mr. Peterson, in his usual role of defender of the public interest, upheld Aletha Urquart, the County Administrator. At the next meeting the malcontent reappeared to be heard again. Under his coat he had two revolvers. He shot and injured Mrs. Urquart, County Commissioner Jerry Rajnus and Board Chairman Fred Peterson. Aging Judge U. E. Reeder dived and caught the legs of the assassin driving him to the floor before he could fire further shots. The three wounded were immediately hospitalized but the subclavian artery of Peterson was severed and he died within minutes. At the trial of the murderer, a skillful lawyer plead insanity and the assassin was committed to the state hospital. He later escaped but Urquart had left town in fear while Jerry Rajnus, although recovered, was partially crippled in one arm. After some time the assassin was recaptured.

A shocked community mourned the death of Fred Peterson but few realized the permanent contribution he had made to Klamath County. One board member, Roy Gienger, said, "He ran the district with his own blood."

When we named a school after him Fred said, "It is quite a responsibility to live up to having a school named for you." He certainly did live up to it and died serving the ideals of the public interest. I, for one, could not imagine a guy like him dying in bed.

CAP COLLIER - THE WARRIOR

The year, 1936 · The scene, University of Oregon, Johnson Hall. We are seated in the lecture room of Dr. Harold Noble, a brilliant lecturer who was an authority on foreign affairs. Such an authority, in fact, that he was called into government service when the United States became involved in World War 2.

The topic of the lecture on this day was the involvement of America in World War I. Our professor called the attention of the class to the rather ridiculous construction of some military trenches on some of the property around the city of Eugene, Oregon. My reaction to the description of this event was the same as the entire class · "How silly can you get?"

The year, 1982 · The scene, in the office of Alfred "Cap" Collier in Klamath Falls, Oregon. Cap was then 89 years old. He said, "I graduated from the University of Oregon in civil engineering in 1914. In 1915, I did engineering work for my uncle Frank McCornack at Caledonia and Wocas Marshes near Klamath Falls."

As I listened to Cap, my thoughts went back to the college lecture and how different a little enlightenment can make a seemingly useless historical event look to the sincere student of history.

World War I, fought mostly on the soil of France, was a long, agonizing period of trench warfare where the soldiers spent months in the mud. New terms were invented such as: doughboys, trench foot, cooties and the most dramatic term "over the top." Americans developed a hatred of the German Kaiser never equaled until Hitler came along. Pictures of spike-helmeted German officers and displays of the inhuman weapons of the Huns helped promote Liberty Bond sales. I recall seeing an exhibit of German weapons showing a type of steel, gravity-propelled darts about five inches long which were to be hand-thrown from aircraft. They were capable of penetrating the steel helmets of the defenseless foot soldiers below.

Cap Collier enlisted in Company D of the Oregon National Guard, a battalion of engineers. They were taken to Fort Lewis near Tacoma, Washington, for training where they laid out sewers. Next he served at Charlotte, North Carolina, for further training in French warfare. In 1918, he volunteered for the U.S. Army and after arriving in France, he trained with the 41st Division. He applied for combat duty and was transferred to the 1st Regiment of the First Division.

Cap said that the U.S. Army was a skeleton organization at first and its duty was to fight with the French under French direction. Germany had been at war with France and England for nearly four years when the U.S. entered the Allied Forces.

One duty of the combat engineers was to construct earth fortifications, trenches and communication trenches. Small military advances were made at a terrible cost for either side.

Cap was a first lieutenant by this time. He said that there were two types of advances: the surprise advance "over the top" and into enemy lines; the other type was preceded by heavy artillery barrage. Observers were put aloft in balloons attached to the ground with cables in order to judge the effectiveness of the artillery. Going over the top in either type of advance was a terrifying experience.

In order to get the men emotionally involved, the officers led out first. Cap said that "each man felt if others could do it, he could." On one occasion Cap said that he had to insist that a frightened soldier hang onto his Sam Brown officer's belt as he entered "No Man's Land."

The Germans felt if they could get close enough to shell Paris, the French would give up. They were close enough to drop a few heavy artillery shells on Paris from the giant "Big Bertha" cannons named after Bertha Krupp.

The French watchword was "They shall not pass." In planning the final advance on Paris, the German Army had constructed a double track railroad and vehicle roads into a narrow penetration point near Soissons, France. This was done in order to transport the enormous amounts of ammunition and supplies. They held high ground on a nearby hill for observation posts from which to direct the final thrust.

By this time, the green American troops had given an excellent account of themselves. Their numbers had increased so the Allied High Command allowed them to have an army of their own under General John J. Pershing, a former cavalry officer.

The Allied Command realized that the German railroad and communications must be cut off if Paris was to be saved. Trench warfare was abandoned and a surprise attack was planned from both east and west. The American 1st Division was given the task of spearheading the attack. General Pershing gave the officers an emotional goodby, telling them that he would not see many of them again.

The former private from Oregon was now Captain Collier. His orders were to construct a bridge across the Couvres River in sixty minutes so the open warfare attack would be a surprise. He said that the only timbers they could find were obtained by tearing down nearby farm buildings. The Yankee engineers made it on time and the attack was on. Thoughts of home came to him as the cavalry crossed the bridge. He knew that many of the horses were from Lake and Klamath counties. Some were probably from Rube Long's roundups.

A cavalry saddle had a special leather holder for the lancer's spear. The spear could be help upright but in an attack it was lowered to skewer the enemy. A well-trained horse was as important as the

GAS!!—A new element, mustard gas, was added by the Germans. This increased the terror of war and had to be countered by protective equipment. The invention of the tank by the British helped change the course of events.

HORSE ROUNDUP IN LAKE COUNTY—When Collier saw the cavalry horses in France, it gave him a feeling of nostalgia as he knew they were raised in the ranges of Lake and Klamath County.

horseman. The spear made a super bayonet that could penetrate any type of protective clothing.

Cutting the German railroads and communications was a near impossible assignment but the Americans did not know it. In the fierce advance on the German positions, the 1st Division was joined by

MUDDY TRENCHES IN FRANCE—The static warfare in mud and misery placed a heavy responsibility on Army Engineers, who had to plan and construct according to the current battle plan.

French Foreign Legion troops, mainly Moroccan and some Senegalese. Cap said they were great fighters. They did not fear death as they believed that if killed in battle they would go directly to heaven. Centuries of desert warfare had taught them that shock could be avoided if they bound up their testicles in a painful position before going into battle.

Another custom of these Sons of Mohammed- they collected human ears! Cap said a small Moraccan officer reported back with a group of German prisoners. When he unrolled his pack a loaf of French bread rolled out and about a dozen human ears. Could this account for the name of the French commanding general "Mangin the Butcher?"

The foreign Legionnaries were relieved and dropped back after two days of fierce fighting. Another American Division composed of abouth fifty percent Marines, including brother Charles Collier, was relieved in three days but the First Division was engaged in combat for five days before being relieved.

Pershing's operation, although costly, was a success. Cut off from their transportation by the English and Americans, the Germans had to burn their supplies to prevent capture. Collier believes this battle stopped the advance, saved Paris and was a turning point in World War I. He was offered the French decoration, The Croix De Guerre, but refused it as his men were not to receive it also.

CAPTAIN COLLIER—Collier wanted to come home following the war. He was however, assigned as road construction supervisor in Germany.

After capturing the small French town of Sedan, the villagers went into the orchards where they had buried their valuables to prevent their confiscation by the Germans. As the Americans watched, the diggers came upon a cache at a depth of about four feet. Digging farther, the main treasure was uncovered at a depth of eight feet. Perhaps the Vikings and Romans taught the French how to survive invasion.

I shall not forget the end of World War I. At the age of ten, I was hunting with my father in the woods. We heard the church bells and the town's fire bell ringing. Walking downtown, we observed the celebration on November 11. Free fireworks were given away by the merchants. In a spectacular display, my cousin Lymon dragged a burning effigy of the Kaiser down the street behind his galloping horse. The armistice meant a great deal to our family as my brother Cecil in the U.S. Navy was on a submarine patrol in the North Sea off Inverness, Scotland.

Following the Armistice, Collier applied for discharge. Instead, he was ordered into Germany for a period where he encountered a new and different kind of problem - getting his men out of bed! They had not slept in beds for so long they were reluctant to leave them.

Collier's combat engineers built roads as well as a skating pond for children. He was selected by his commander as head of a guard of honor to meet the first army commander. When Pershing asked Cap what they wanted, he asked only for warm socks for his men.

In battle, a loyalty and spirit seems to develop between effective officers and those in their command. One officer from World War II told me that it was like a football squad if the officer and the morale of his troops was good.

Alfred Collier was born December 14, 1892. At the time of my recorded interview, he was 89 years old. I was tremendously impressed with the military experience he revealed to me. Could it be possible that this Klamath County man has such a key role in the final stages of World War One? A look at the history book European Civilization and Politics Since 1815 by Erick Achorn quoting from page 446: "The position of honor on the right (General) Foch intrusted to Pershing's First Army. The American field of operations was the most difficult terrain on the entire front, the Argonne Forest, where in over four years the French had been unable to make any impression. Owing to the vital strategic importance of the Argonne, as well, any threat here was bound to meet strong resistance. To Pershing fell the honor of opening the combined offensive-----Casualties were ten percent."

Yes, Cap's story was correct. Anyone around Eugene for digging trenches?

HENRY SEMON
The Man Who Loved The Soil

Catlow Valley is one of the loneliest places in Oregon. It lies east of Hart Mountain on a flat desert once covered by an ancient lake. The only reason for a person to go there would be because of his work or his love for the desert.

Malcom Epley and Henry Semon loved the desert. These men were very different yet they made a great team. Mac Epley, who told me this story was 120 percent journalist. Coming out of the University of Oregon, he became editor of the Klamath Herald-News under publisher Frank Jenkins. Mac later advanced as editor of a Long Beach, California newspaper but he never could stay away from the smell of sagebrush and retired to live in Fort Bidwell. He told me with pride that he had been accepted by the natives of Modoc County and was allowed to sit on a bench at the back of the Cedarville Store. Epley was Herald-News editor at the time of the incident.

It was early in the 1930's when Henry Semon and Epley took part in the annual ceremonies of The Order of the Antelope. Semon had been elevated to the order's highest honor "Chief White Tail." Neither man had been long enough in the desert air so they decided to drive down the long sloping road on the east side of Hart Mountain Antelope Refuge. The adventurers reached the flat dusty bed of Catlow Valley before discovering that Henry's Buick was out of gas. It was many miles from the nearest gasoline in Blitzen. The two sat disconsolately wondering what to do when they saw dust rising on the desert floor toward the north. As it came closer they could discern a model A Ford. Both stepped out to meet and greet Dr. Luther Cressman, head of the anthropology department at the University of Oregon. Along with his assistant, Cressman was doing archaeological research along the shores of the dried lake where the ancient Indians had lived.

Cressman's offer to help came soon. He offered to tow them in if Semon had a tow chain or rope. Nothing in the trunk, not even an old tire chain. The group finally decided to remove the battery cable from the Buick and attach it to the back of Cressman's model A. Luck was with the Klamath men. It was almost miraculous for a traveler to be in Catlow Valley. Now they had the solution to their problem. Starting out slowly, then gaining speed they came to an unusually dusty spot in the trail. When the dust reached the point that Henry could see nothing he hit the brakes. The battery cable broke! Again they were in trouble.

Mac Epley did not tell me of the conversation that followed which is just as well. I had taken classes from Cressman. He is not a patient man, neither was Henry. Somehow they were able to patch up the cable and cross the desert to Blitzen.

When I first heard of Henry Semon, I was a teacher in the Altamont School District and he was a County School Board member. After my work took me to Henley, his son Charlie was a student there and I became acquainted with Henry, known as Hank to his neighbors. I was impressed by the respect and admiration that community people had for Mr. Semon. He was not big, not handsome and especially he was not a good speaker. His way of emphasizing a sentence was to wave his arm with two fingers extended. Other qualities which more than compensated for his lack of speech-making skills were his intelligence, courage, integrity and social adaptability.

He was born at Port Clinton, Ohio, in 1884, son of Thomas and Louise Semon. Henry inherited the German work ethic of his immigrant parents. He became an expert carpenter and in 1906 left Ohio to follow this trade in Los Angeles and Bisbee, Arizona. Later he and his wife Hazel purchased the farm which lies about one mile south of the Henley School. It was here that he established his reputation as a skillful farmer and business manager.

When County Extension Agent Charlie Henderson brought in a test cargo of certified netted gem seed potatoes from Idaho in 1922, Mr. Semon was one of those selected to grow and certify the seed. He proved to be a good example for others leading to a multi-million dollar industry in the Klamath Basin. His interest in agriculture never lessened and the productivity of his farm has been maintained to this day.

At the urging of his neighbors and friends, Semon filed for the State Legislature in 1932 as a Democrat. When he arrived at the state capitol, his looks and speech betrayed his rural background. Lobbyists who sought to take advantage of him soon learned that beneath the exterior was a keen mind and strong character that could neither be conned or coerced. Respect for his ability grew so rapidly that after Oregon's capitol burned in 1935, Governor Charles Martin appointed Semon to the Capitol Building Committee where his talent as a builder proved so valuable.

He was a sociable fellow and one concerned about public affairs. His membership in the Henley Grange was expanded to include the Elks, Rotary Club and Chamber of Commerce in which body he served on the board of directors.

Semon's election to the state legislature became a matter of routine. His friend, Epley of the News-Herald faithfully kept the public informed and Semon's influence in the legislative body became a legend.

Today membership on the Joint Ways and Means Committee is

131

THE CAR THAT SAVED EPLEY—Luther Cressman (left), head of the Anthropology Dept. at University of Oregon, stands with graduate student, Howard Stafford, in a 1932 photo. Cressman did pioneer research in Oregon archaeology but it took years, until the development of radio-carbon dating, before his discoveries were recognized.

MALCOLM "MAC" EPLEY— Former editor of the Klamath Herald News and Long Beach Press Telegram. Mac loved the Klamath country and could never get enough of the smell of sagebrush. After retirement from the Long Beach editorship, he moved with his wife Jane to Fort Bidwell in Modoc County. Here he took pride in being allowed "to sit" with others in the back of the general store in Cedarville.

regarded as a great political reward. Few seats are given to minority party members. Respect for Semon was so great that he was repeatedly given chairmanship of the powerful committee even when opposition Republicans had complete control. Even with the complexities and problems of a state budget, he never lost his interest in

LEGISLATOR SEMON—
Quick intelligence, a great
sense of humor and un-
questioned loyalty made him
one of the most powerful
men in the state legislature
for a long period of years.

THE MOST SOPHISTICATED HAY-
SEED IN OREGON—At Lakeview,
Henry Semon poses in his favorite
garb after being elected "Chief
White Tail" in the Order of
Antelope. It can be seen that
friends have stuffed a little hay in
the top of his shoe to make him
feel at home. Semon never hunted
but loved to fish salmon in the
Umpqua River.

agriculture nor his memory of the value of his training as a carpenter.

In the budgeting process he became well acquainted with Oscar Paulson, State Director of Vocational Education. Oscar was a former agriculture teacher who never lost his common touch with farmers. He dreamed of establishing regional vocational schools. Henry discussed this proposal with me and I did not favor it as I was in public school work and at that time there was no such thing as state basic school support funds. My opinion probably had little effect upon the legislator but another event did.

During the War with Japan in the South Pacific, many American marines contracted tropical diseases which were unusual and for which there seemed no effective treatment. The victims had malaria and filariasis. Some Navy doctors were acquainted with the altitude and climate in Klamath Falls and, as a result, a medical treatment center, the Marine Barracks, was built high on a hill above the city where Navy uniforms became commonplace while the carrier pilots of Gruman Wildcats and Hellcats were being trained at the local airport. Now Marine uniforms were visible about the town and county. Soon the tropical disease program was a huge success. The war was over and while many Leathernecks returned to their hometowns, many stayed and made homes in Klamath.

An empty building is a dangerous thing whether it is an old armory, hotel, geriatric center or marine barracks, there is an almost uncontrollable public urge to fill it with something. Thus the old government buildings at Vanport were converted to a college later to become Portland State University. So the Marine Barracks attracted the attention of Oscar Paulson and Henry Semon. Marshall Cornett was the influential President of the Oregon Senate and Earl Smith was Governor. Winston Purvine, a member of Paulson's staff in the Department of Vocational Education, was designated as head of the new Oregon vocational school.

Another historical event took place which had a marked effect on Henry Semon. His only son, Charles, who had played on my football team at Henley, joined and advanced in the U.S. military to become a lieutenant in the paratroops. On D Day, June 6, 1944, the allied forces attacked Hitler's German Army in Europe. Lieutenant Charles Semon leading his men jumped while loaded with grenades and weapons. The navigator had made an error. Charlie landed in the waters of the Zeider Zee and was never seen again.

This death cast a pall of grief over the Semon family which now included only the mother Hazel and sister Gretchen, now Mrs. Wallace Thompson. The man who was always ready for a good time or fight became more gentle and introspective. In 1955 he was still influential and always ready to help solve the problems of the school district

LT. CHARLES SEMON—A 1938 graduate of Henley High School, Semon became an officer in the Paratroops.

where I was serving as superintendent.

Henry felt uncomfortable being a Democrat but not a liberal. He told me that he was receiving a lot of distasteful comment from some of his party colleagues so he decided to change his party registration to Independent. Epley had gone to Long Beach· Semon's great service was mostly forgotten. He was defeated by two Democrats, Carl Yancey and John Kerbow.

As one last valuable permanent community effort, he wanted to construct a new church to honor the memory of the Henley boys who had lost their lives in World War 2. It was my pleasure to give him some small help in planning this. My best moment came later though when I was invited to be dedication speaker for Semon Hall at Oregon Technical Institute where I told them about the tough little man who shook his two fingers so influentially over the government of Oregon.

Other buildings were named for Governor Snell and Cornett. Naturally, Semon Hall was the big shop building where students learn-ed to use their hands.

THE DAY THE MULLET INDUSTRY WAS SAVED

When Sam Ritchey called he said, "We have something we want you to come and look at. We don't know what it is. It's over on an island in Lost River." I've always been a sucker to go on "wild goose chases" so I agreed to accompany Sam and Keith Read, County Park Director, on an investigative tour.

I was picked up early to avoid a windy trip. Our boat was put in at the ramp below the long bridge on the Crystal Springs road. Our trip was to take us up-river to an island called, of all things, "Sam Ritchey Island." I was not aware that it had been named for Sam and then made into a county park. Two outdoor toilets with the doors torn off were the only things that marred the otherwise natural scene.

I followed Sam and Read. Here and there, fragments of obsidian indicated that Indians had occupied the island. This caused my adrenalin to flow as I thought we were nearing some archaeological feature. At last my guides pointed down. There appeared to be a row of rocks all in a straight line. This was highly unusual because Indians rarely used rocks in building their habitations and, when they did, circles were used instead of straight line features.

I excitedly started to uncover the row of stones. Soon to my chagrin brick was turned up. Could Indians bake bricks? Another fragment of brick appeared, then off to one side a piece of iron. We were able to trace the foundation wall for several feet. My memory went back to a story I had been told by Adah Grigsby Brown some years before. We had made an archaeological discovery in the modern interpretation of the term. We had found the site of the Lost River Mullet Cannery near Olene.

A man from Medford had built the cannery in 1892 before the Horseshoe Dam was built to divert the Lost River waters into the Klamath River. They both canned and dried the fish according to Mrs. Brown. I understand the venture closed even before the dam structure stopped the annual fish run from Tule Lake. Perhaps it was due to the single, short seasonal fishing opportunity or perhaps the fish were not tasty enough to be commercially valuable. Finding the remains of the old structure did not end my bout with the problems of mullet.

It seems that a cousin of the Lost River mullet, which had spring spawning runs up the Williamson and past Chiloquin, was causing problems for the Game Commission. The over abundance of the fish made them so easy to catch that waste was occurring as fishermen would snag more than they could use, then leave them on the shores to putrefy and attract flies, worms and dogs. In their wisdom, the Game Commission decided to make them less easy to catch. How?

WILLIAMSON RIVER MULLET—Mullet were called Tsu'am by Klamath Indians. The mullet is not a pretty fish but was a major food source for the Klamath Indians over the centuries along the Williamson River.

-simply make them a game fish and illegal to snag. The lawmakers, always ready to help in conservation movements, passed the law.

It was discovered, come time for the next mullet run, (The Indians always called them suckers.) that the mullet does not bite like trout, chub or salmon. The only way to catch them is to snag them with a triple hook or a gaff hook. Police officers and game officers found it hard to explain to Indians, whose ancestors and their ancestors had moved to the mullet runs for centuries, that they could no longer spear and snag the suckers. Actually, few if any, Klamath Indians were dependent upon fish in 1961. The fish were, however, quite edible if properly prepared.

Since I had never been an avid mullet fisherman, the nature of the problem was only discovered when I arrived at the 1961 Legislative Assembly as a freshman legislator. My colleagues, Senator Boivin and Representative George Flitcraft, and I decided to meet the problems head-on and look after the needs of our constituents. Ordinarily when confronted with such a problem, one looks for others who have a similar problem. Unfortunately, Klamath, which is unique in many ways, was the only county whose streams supported mullet runs. This meant that the voting score in the House would be 58 to 2 and 29 to 1 in the Senate in favor of those who could care less about the mullet but had other problems in which they badly needed help. With the encouragement and support of the Game Commission the three of us decided to co-sponsor the bill to legalize the snagging of mullet.

When you arrive as a freshman legislator, you first learn the customs. One of these was that the majority party gets first choice of the available seats on the House floor. In those days, this was your only office, your conference room and the desk of your secretary. Within

137

the seats left for the minority Republicans, seniority next prevailed. This left Flitcraft and Howe at the bottom of the pecking order.

George was lucky. He drew a seat in the back row near the telephone and water cooler. In that position one could leave the floor unobtrusively without attracting any attention. Nicely settled in the new haven, he soon discovered that his seat was next to Representative Grace Peck of Portland. This lady was willing to speak at length on almost any bill, especially if it concerned the fishing industry or welfare. She also kept a supply of containers holding candy which she dispensed freely to legislators, lobbyists and visitors. Worst of all for George, she loved flowers and kept her desk stacked with all varieties. Now George, a victim of hay fever, could not stand the flowers. I don't know how he persuaded the Speaker, Bob Duncan, to trade seats with him. He must have been red-eyed and sobbing but Duncan gave him a seat in the very front row of the House chamber where you get the most attention.

Now unfortunately George had another weakness or perhaps it was a strength. Anyway he could not stand endless and useless oratory. He studied his bills and did his homework. Each morning he, like most of us, had decided how to vote on the measures called third readings which were to come before the House. As the debate and oratory proceeded, it would sometimes go beyond the point of his tolerance and he would leave, perhaps feigning the need to visit the restroom. Since the speaker system was connected to the back of the House floor he could always return when the roll call vote was taken. His departure and returns were easily observable from the prominent place in the front. These events did not always meet with favor, especially by those delivering the long-winded speeches, who were sure that they could pick up that one vote needed for passage of the bill.

As the session proceeded, the time for committee hearings on the mullet bill became near. I was able to persuade George that he was younger and more of a sportsman than I, therefore, best fitted to appear at the committee hearings as an advocate. He was assured that the Game Commission would be at his side.

After the Fish and Game Committee sent the bill to the floor with a "do pass" fellow members, who saw our names as sponsors of the bill, began to ask insincere and demeaning questions about the fish and the sport of mullet fishing in general.

The day arrived to carry the bill. Carry, means to speak as an advocate and try to persuade affirmative votes. Finally George arose to speak. We both knew the sale of triple hooks and gaff hooks would be devastated if we failed. As he began his presentation within one minute there were only three legislators on the floor- George, the

MAYOR GEORGE FLIT-CRAFT—State Representative George Flitcraft taken in 1961. After serving three terms in the legislature, he was active in fraternal work. He has been mayor of Klamath Falls since 1975.

Speaker and Howe. The speech was, of course, brief. When it was over, the members returned to their desks and passed the bill over-whelmingly. George was a popular guy in spite of his low tolerance for oratory. We both knew that when the bill reached the Senate it would be in good hands· that Boivin was a man who knew something about mullet.

KLAMATH'S FIRST RECREATION PROGRAM

Economic conditions were bad and getting worse in 1932. The United States was in the beginning o f a long depression. In Klamath Falls a campaign was on to promote the use of wooden boxes. Merchants were encouraged, and even pressured, to order their goods shipped in wooded boxes. This movement was designed to protect the jobs of the men and women who worked in the several box factories in the locality.

In the presidential campaign, the eloquence and wit of Franklin D. Roosevelt was first brought into play. He successfully pictured Herbert Hoover as the villain in the economic downturn. Roosevelt's leadership swept a great many Democrats into power on both the local and national level.

One such person, a rather handsome and articulate man from Washington, came to Klamath Falls and was rather easily persuaded to run for mayor. This was Willis Mahoney. He had arrived in town too late to establish a legal residence and get his name printed on the ballot so a write-in campaign was conducted. The fervor of his followers was aroused by attacks on the power company called Cop-

WILLIS MAHONEY IN 1933— As mayor of Klamath Falls, he was very active. He established a strong political base and was nominated by the Democrat Party for U.S. Senator.

(Courtesy of Mary Jane Van Dusen)

co. This was a logical political choice as few people enjoy paying power and water bills. One proposal in the campaign was to bring the cool, clean waters of Spring Creek down to a municipally-owned utility. After many speeches, even a torchlight parade, Willis Mahoney was swept into office as mayor in a write-in campaign.

By 1933 the mayor appointed a City Recreation Committee made up of leading citizens to develop and supervise a recreation program. I was recommended by Fred Peterson as a supervisor to share the job with Ella Redkey, a young physical education graduate of the University of Oregon. The plan was to be financed by popular subscription. My salary was to be fifty dollars per month with the provision that I furnish my own car and expenses. This did not sound like much money even in a depression but the alternative was nothing. Besides, I could establish my reputation as a youth leader and my services would be in great demand.

Ella was to have the girl's program at Fremont School. A number of young women, who wanted to become teachers, volunteered to serve without pay for the girl's program. Among them were Lois Rumer, Beth Cummings and Lillian Redkey.

Handicrafts and physical activity were carried on. Joe Peake, School Physical Education Supervisor, loaned us the equipment to carry out the program.

ELLA REDKEY IN 1932—Miss Redkey had a long and successful career as a teacher of physical education in the Klamath Union High School.

AIR-COOLED FRANKLIN—The car that was sacrificed in the name of recreation. Standing by the car, dressed for adventure, is Alice Applegate Peil, daughter of O. C. "Cap" Applegate. It was probably an adventure to travel in this vehicle especially on the roads built in those days.

(Odell Collection)

The boys were to meet at Modoc Field in the afternoon to get exercise and have fun. In the first turnouts we had a sizeable group of boys who had been attracted by the publicity. There was a wide range of ages but such activities as softball, speed ball and calisthenics were carried on. It wasn't long until the numbers of participants declined. I soon discovered that the boys of Klamath Falls were too smart to exert themselves in the heat in the middle of the day. My suggestion to the committee that an evening program be tried was rejected.

Another inspiration of mine was tried, however- a camp cookery program. Frank Sexton, County 4-H Club Leader, provided the materials and a goodly number of boys turned out at Moore Park. A shady section was set aside for the cookery project. Since no water was available, any dish washing had to be done at home. When most of the young cooks were about three-fourths through the required part of the cookery, a disaster occurred. The piney woods, where the rock-ringed fires were laid, caught fire and burned the entire area that had been set aside for the program. We never knew whether the burn resulted from left-over sparks or if some ambitious cook decided to try some extracurricular work. Frank Sexton always wondered why only four boys completed the cookery requirements when so many had enrolled.

After the recreation program was about one month along the committee decided that we should try some vocational training. One of the group had contacted Lou Arens, owner of the Plymouth car distribution agency, who offered his shop as a training area. A mechanic was found who would donate his time, then the aspiring auto mechanics were notified. Several of the older boys, who neither liked to cook or play baseball in the sun, showed up. When I arrived at Lou's garage with the boys, we found that someone had generously donated an air-cooled Franklin automobile. I suspect that it was the only air-cooled motor ever in Klamath County until the introduction of the Volkswagon thirty years later. The zealous young mechanics eagerly tore into the Franklin and in about three sessions had completely demolished and destroyed it. I asked Julian Eccles what the value of such a car would be today and he said about $15,000 to $20,000.

Apparently, the girl's program at Fremont conducted by Miss Redkey was going smoothly for we were requested by the committee to prepare a float for the 4th of July parade. I was at a loss for examples of my work- certainly a burned forest or a demolished car would not do.

Mrs. Early of the committee had persuaded someone to provide a truck and Ella's volunteers and participants did an excellent job of preparing the float. When it rolled down main street, it was loaded with handsome smiling youngsters holding proudly the tools of their trade and products of their training. They had puppets and handicrafts but mostly bats, baseballs, basketballs and volleyballs, all property of the city school district. Along each side of the truck was a large banner "City Recreation Program." Who could doubt the value and wisdom of an effort like this.

As the hot dog-days of August approached, the male youths of the city showed less and less enthusiasm for physical activities. Also, it was more difficult to find donors who wanted to use their limited resources for the program. There was only enough money left to pay one salary. I was confronted then with an easy choice. I could either go out and try to raise more money or let Ella receive the last month's pay. I took the noble course and resigned. Even though fifty dollars was fifty dollars, the sun was hot and the fish were biting.

Despite dire predictions to the contrary, Willis Mahoney proved to be a good mayor. He was reelected, then became a power in the state democratic party. Nominated for the U.S. Senate, he suffered a narrow defeat. He was later appointed to an important post in Japan by Franklin D. Roosevelt.

Lou Arens was appointed to the State Industrial Accident Commission about 1938 where he served for many years. I'm not sure that my resignation contributed to the success of these men but I believe it helped.

143

SIN CITY
AND THE RECREATION FUND

The year is 1954: the month February. A bandit is shot by a policeman as he is robbing at gunpoint, a madam and the girls who worked as prostitutes on Broad Street. Worse yet, it is discovered that the madam was paying for police protection into a city fund, No. 307, called the Improvement Fund. Half the citizens of Klamath Falls are aghast and outraged. Half say, "So what's new?"

The following self-righteous editorial appeared in the Portland Oregon Journal on February 15, 1954:

Strange Deal at Klamath Falls

When 10 Klamath Falls ministers issued a statement concerning the existence of organized vice in their city, it might have been expected that city officials would hit the ceiling and deny the charges. That's what always happens in Portland. (One clever Portland mayor put the complaining pastors on a committee to "help" him clean up Portland.)

But "bitter denials" and "blistering retorts" didn't fill the air at Klamath Falls. No, sir! There were instead frank admissions that "houses of prostitution had existed in Klamath Falls for 25 years." More than that, too. The mayor frankly admitted "an improvement fund" was started in 1949 by city ordinance, establishing a depository for contributions from bawdy houses and slot machines.

If you can't lick 'em, join 'em!

What upset this pleasant arrangement, by which the city council profited from its partnership with vice, was the regrettable publicity which followed when a gunman was killed by police as he tried to hold up a madam and her girls. The bandit's lack of finesse was shocking. Such direct action was strictly illegal. The bandit's methods did not have the sanction of city ordinance such as the city's illegal split with the vice dens. But, come to think of it, the robbery is no more illegal than is prostitution and organized gambling.

Well, a new Klamath county district attorney is one of those old-fashioned fellows who regards his oath to enforce the laws as binding. He complained to the mayor that this little deal with vice and crime had to stop. The mayor reportedly told the madams and gaming proprietors that they were no longer to contribute to the "improvement fund."

Attorney General Thornton, who some months ago reported that there are organized prostitution circuits in the state and they must be cleaned up, issued a statement commending the Klamath county DA for "your fearless and upright stand. You may quote me as 100 per cent behind your enforcement program."

There the matter stands. But it is interesting what the money was used for when appropriated from the "improvement fund." It appears to have built a municipal swimming pool and other worth-while civic projects.

City officials assert Klamath Falls citizens appeared to a p p r o v e the partnership with the local vice magnates.

Of course there may have been some ignorant of existence of such a fund. It wasn't phrased in terms to admit partnership with prostitution and gambling. It spoke only of "Account No. 307" which was a catchall for cash and anonymous legacies and gifts. But those "in the know" understood that someone from each of the city's principal bawdy houses waltzed in each month with a "legacy" of $200. Slot machines, illegal under Oregon's constitution since 1859, which outlawed gambling, paid $10 a month. There is no statement that madams and gambling chiefs failing to trot in with their "legacies" were subject to arrest, but it is assumed that the Klamath Falls police had to have some reason for donning stars and uniforms. If they were not hired to enforce the laws, at least they could collect for the 'improvement fund."

Public officials with regard for the sanctity of their oaths of office will never make a covenant with purveyors of vice and crime.

Oregon Journal   *9
MONDAY, FEB. 15, 1954

Apparently, sin was not new in the city by the lakes. Ida Moymer Odell who worked in the bank made these observations:

"The little town was seething with activity during our first years here. There had never been a payroll, as it was long before the advent of the lumbering industry. So when Ericksen and Peterson, who were the contractors for building the roadbed for the Southern Pacific, paid off their many road hands by check and at the same time the United States Reclamation Service was constructing the big canal from Upper Klamath Lake paid off their sizeable crew of workmen, these two payrolls were the first of any moment to bolster the business of the town. It is sad to say that a great proportion of the Ericksen and Peterson checks reached the bank by the Redlight District. The Madams would bring the checks in by the handfuls, cash them and go to their safety deposit boxes. They were not in the habit of having bank accounts. An occasional wave of purity would hit our city government and arrests would be made. One of the most famous arrests was that of "Diamond Dick" the lady proprietor of one of these houses. Diamond Dick did not remain in custody very long, but while she did, some of our prominent business men seemed to be walking on a live bed of coals and they succeeded in getting her released - at her request - if request is the proper term for the pressure put upon them. She left town as soon as she was released.

"At that time this part of the community was isolated from the town by a marshy piece of land behind, approximately what is now South Sixth Street between Plum and Commercial. There was an inlet from the lake which was spanned by a narrow wooden bridge called "The Bridge of Sighs." Across this bridge were the several large places which housed the girls. One of these houses was called The Old Iron Door, and was later moved to Spring Street when that unsavory district was closed out. From what I have heard, The Old Iron Door continued to conduct the same type of business.

"Well, one morning as soon as the bank opened a swarm of girls from the wrong side of the Bridge of Sighs flocked in with Ericksen and Peterson checks to cash, and upon receiving the money headed for the S.P.R.R. Station and took the next train out. The body of one of the construction gang had been found floating in the little inlet on the lakeside of the Bridge of Sighs and the Madams wanted no part of an investigation, so shepherded their flocks out of town."

Sam Walker, who served as the town's police officer in the early days, told me that the city's jail was located down in the tules that extended from Lake Ewauna. So when he arrested someone in town, he could get along with them all right until he started to lead them through the tules to the jail. "Then I would sometimes have to whip them in order to get them to the jail because they thought I was taking

KLAMATH FALLS 1911—Lake Ewauna was once called "Chiny Lake" after a Chinaman who had a business there. A short canal can be seen extending toward 6th Street.

them down to the lake to drown them." (It's a good thing for Sam the A.C.L.U. was not yet invented.)

J. Paul Matthews was serving as city auditor at the time Fund 307 was established. His explanation of the conditions surrounding the action make the city fathers, if not lily-white, a least a little more reasonable then the Journal editorial writer pictured them. Paul said, "There were few places available for working men in those days. Places such as Astoria, Coos Bay and Bend, as well as Klamath Falls, had a high tolerance level for sin."

I can remember when the Klamath Billiards on main street was a kind of clubhouse for loggers and lumberjacks. In the back, a horse parlor operated openly where bets could be placed. There were, of course, pool tables and card tables. Matthews said that "at one card table pimps gathered each day to play a card game called pangigni. Rumor had it that their rank and prestige was indicated by the number of buttons on the cuffs of their tailor-made shirts. Each button for one girl."

When Ashurst was elected circuit judge, having received complaints from housewives about gambling losses of their husbands, he asked the grand jury to look into gambling charges. As a result, a twenty-five cent limit was ordered by the jury placed on any bets at local card rooms.

At that time, it was the custom for houses of prostitution to pay

CITY HALL—This building served as fire station, court and administrative building. Except for the fire truck ramp, it appears much the same today.

(Odell Collection)

law enforcement officers under the table for protection. Some of the larger houses would bring a check for $250 each month to the city hall. Paul said that council members did not know what to do with the money. In 1938 they decided to establish a fund for such gifts called the Improvement fund. They stopped all illegal protection payments by the Madams and ordered a $250 monthly payment from the five major houses. In addition, they required a ten dollar monthly fee for each slot machine. Paul explained that police chief Keith Ambrose was "strictly honest and had never received an illegal payment of protection money."

The council's agreement provided for an element of control as well as protection for the safety of the prostitutes. This system worked until the Navy established a base here in 1942. They informed city officials that if prostitution did not cease the city would be placed "off limits" to Navy personnel. The order was, of course, for protection of the health of the personnel. Immediately all houses were closed and the order enforced.

It was not long after the Navy base closed that the "oldest profession" was again practiced and payments into the voluntary Improvement Account No. 307 resumed. The funds were eventually expended for playgrounds and parks. Paul said that the city acquired some property in the hot water area of Main Street where the municipal swimming pool was built.

In 1954, when the bandit tried to holdup the Madam at a Broad Street address, police were summoned and the robber was shot by a policeman, the district attorney named Alderson was outraged to discover that prostitution existed and that payments were being made into the city coffers. Even the State Attorney General managed to take advantage of the publicity value by denouncing the crime.

Sin City again became lily-white where I suppose it remains today.

ANDY COLLIER -
GENEROUS SCOTSMAN

It is Sunday, 1913: The crew of the big dredge Klamath Queen is at lunch as she sits on the waters of the Upper Klamath Lake. On Board on this day are E. P. McCornack, owner of the Queen. Also, a visitor sharing the Sunday dinner is a young man recently graduated from the University of Oregon, Andrew Collier, nephew of the boat's owner. Business graduate Collier is currently working one of the windows in the First National Bank at 4th and Main Street. At the table sits Jack Linman, roustabout, who operates the supply boat. Jack said that the old gentleman inquired, "Andrew, how are things going at the bank?" The reply, "very fine, Uncle." Then he asked, "Are you saving any money?" "By the time I pay for my room, board and laundry, there is not much left from my forty dollar a month salary." E. P. then said, with a sly wink toward Linman, " No matter what, if you don't save a little, the key to success is not in you."

Andrew did indeed prove that he had the key to success both before and after the dinner on the Klamath Queen. Mac Epley, an Oregon graduate and editor of the Klamath Herald-News, wrote about Collier in 1949 when Collier was named First Citizen of Klamath Falls:

"Eugene born, the fourth of five sons and a daughter, Coller grew up in the Willamette Valley. In 1909 at the age of eighteen, he enrolled in the University of Oregon in the school of business administration. Here began a career that has to this day left its mark on the Oregon campus.

"Karl Onthank '13, one of Collier's classmates, tabs him as 'quiet but extremely effective.' During their junior year, Collier and Onthank, were co-operators of the Oregana, which at that time was put out by the members of the junior class. Onthank was editor, Collier business manager. It was under this regime that the annual got the look it has today - a large, handsome yearbook. The following year the twosome took over the same position on the Emerald, which was at that time a semi-weekly paper. Under Andy Collier's management the paper was able to gather enough business to become a tri-weekly and oftentimes it was put out every day of the week.

"Collier was a member of the Friars, active in the YMCA, was a member of the 1913 doubles handball championship team, ran on the cross country team and was a member of the Oregon club - an independent organization."

On another day, August 3, 1966 more than fifty years after the dinner on the boat, I am with Andy Collier near the bluffs above the Tule Lake Basin. He had taken me there to show me the Indian pictographs, which he, Captain O. C. Applegate and Bert Thomas had

ANDY COLLIER WITH AUTHOR—For fifty years, Andy kept the secret of the location of the Indian petroglyphs near Tule Lake. He feared vandalism would occur if the site was revealed.

found before roads had been built into the region. Their discovery was made by accident when they were walking toward the lake from their camp at Fleener's Chimneys.

Andy looked with pride across the vast Tule Lake Basin toward Malin where he said he had been active in selling land to the settlers coming into the basin from the East.

E. P. McCornack, J. Frank Adams, Rufus Moore and he had formed the Lakeside Land Company. Collier was serving as secretary for the company and was active in sales. Much of the townsite of Malin at that time was under water as well as much farm land. They had six or seven thousand acres which sold for $35. an acre, nothing down.

The dam at Clear Lake and the diversion channel on the Lost River Slough near Henley would soon uncover the rich lake bed for farming. The Adams irrigation works would bring water from the Lower Klamath Lake to the new settlers.

The land company sold six or seven thousand acres of dry land to Bill Dalton for seven dollars an acre. Much of this was brought into production later by the installation of pumps.

Collier said that the Bohemian migrants were very successful farmers, "They built small houses and big barns."

History tells us that the First National Bank progressed suc-

149

cessfully. Andy became vice president and later, a director. At Christian Endeavor he met a young teacher from Iowa, Georgia Porter. They were married in 1916. Georgia said that her spouse was impatient with his progress in Klamath Falls and asked to be transferred to the Merrill branch where he became president at the age of 29. In this capacity, he was able to perform a valuable service to the same people who had bought land from him in earlier years.

In the depression of 1921, the Malin bank failed but Andy persuaded his directors to guarantee the savings of the depositors in the bank that failed.

Of the many successful business ventures, perhaps the most outstanding story of initiative and success was his venture into the cold storage business. In the early days, farmers in the area would saw blocks of ice from the surface of Lost River and Klamath Falls residents obtained ice from the Upper Klamath Lake. Stored and covered with sawdust, the ice would last most of the summer. To utilize the advantage of the cold winter, the Klamath Ice and Storage Company was formed with partners O. C. Carter and Frank Fleet. Andy bought into the company and became president in 1919.

As deliveries progressed, complaints from doctors were recieved about the flora and fauna contained in the naturally-formed ice. After this the machinery was installed to manufacture ice from the city's pure water. College boys found summer employment delivering the ice for home use. The biggest consumer, however, was the railroad company which used vast amounts in the refrigerator cars hauling produce.

The progress of the company was not always smooth. In a letter to his mother Janet McCornack Collier in Eugene, Andy wrote in the summer of 1930:

"The miracle happened again and God came out on my side, pushing me forward to success. The Ewauna Lumber burned about 12 million feet, the biggest fire I ever saw. This adjoined our storage house and platform. There seemed no possibility of saving our storage house and 3,000 tons of ice in it. Alfred and I looked over and practically gave it up. But we put a man on top with a small hose and the Railroad Company ran an engine in with a tank car giving us one line to play on our storage house, and one on lumber nearby.

"Alfred and I monopolized one nozzle and fought the fire but whenever my building smoked and showed signs of going we moved the hose completely along it. The heat was terrific, could be felt for a mile from the fire. Alfred sure was fine on the nozzle. I struggled along trying to keep my lips wet and my heart going. But he merely screwed up his mouth like he was going "over the top" and never hesitated. By a miracle the wind veered and we came slowly out of the heat after

GRANDSON ANDREW WITH PATRIARCH GEORGE COL-LIER—A native of Scotland, George was a professor of physics at the University of Oregon. The house he built on the campus is now used for the Faculty Club.

an hour and a half struggle. Two hundred and fifty feet of the icing platform was burned, ignited purely by the heat of the fire 200 feet away. But we wired them to send on their trains as usual, and while the fire was still burning we iced a train, doing it largely by hand power.

"If the building and platform had burned it would have spoiled our game for this season, but enough of the platform was left to handle the present business and immediate action by Railroad officials will prepare the platform so we can use the whole half mile of platform for icing the Medford pears which begin coming August 5. We are also spending $4,000 this week installing a larger machine in our ice plant, which will enable us to sell 12,000 more tons of ice to the Railroad this summer. Our bottling plant and the ice plant have been running full capacity, and it looks like they would for the next two months.

"I have a crew of Hobos in the Bunkhouse. They are a study, some good, some talkers, some getting away from wives, etc. But we find some pretty square shooters. I put in a hot and cold shower for them the other day and they sure appreciate it."

BORROWED BOXING GLOVES—Andrew showed promise of being a good business man at an early age. Here he joyfully pummels his brother with boxing gloves he had thoughtfully bought for his mother's birthday present.

As refrigeration machinery improved, new purposes for cold storage were found. The plant at Tule Lake was built with Ross Ragland as manager. It is now common practice to hold potatoes in cold storage well into the summer months.

The greatest use now for cold storage is for "in transit" storage. This means a temporary holding place for food items until the market will absorb them.

The little company that delivered algae-laden ice had gone a long way according to a Herald-News item:

"Klamath Falls became one of the largest storage-in-transit points for food products in the Western United States in the fall of 1968 when Klamath Ice and Storage activated its new $250,000 plant.

"Completion of the new storage facility, which holds some 15 million pounds of frozen foods, increased the company's total refrigerated warehouse space from 45 million to 60 million pounds, of which about 15 million is for nonfrozen items such as canned goods and potatoes.

"A six-mile network of oil pipes under the building is controlled by Donald Nabakowski, chief engineer for 25 years."

Meanwhile, the amazing Andy had purchased a farm in the Pine Grove region and named it Anabaglish after the Collier family-seat in Scotland and was experimenting with dry land and sprinkler-irrigated crops.

Georgia and Andy Collier in retirement.

His business judgement had become so respected that he was elected to the board of directors of Equitable Savings and Loan, a statewide firm with headquarters in Portland.

Success in business did not keep Collier or his wife Georgia from doing valuable public service. He served in the Oregon State Legislature in the days (1925-31) when it was a financial sacrifice to do so. In this capacity he helped to establish the Southern Oregon Normal School at Ashland when there was no other educational institution south of Eugene.

During his two terms as president of the Klamath County Chamber of Commerce, the slogan "An Empire Awakening" was adopted and great progress was made in forest protection, agricultural development and highway construction.

In writing a list of public service activities, it is easy to list them but when consideration is given to the meaning of the work, financial assistance, and hours of time donated, it seems amazing that they could be crowded into the lifetime of an already busy man.

I doubt if anyone actually knows of all these works Andy was involved in but here are some additional services: Silver Beaver Award for Boy Scouts, Klamath County Relief Committee, years on the Salvation Army Board, City Planning and Recreation Committee, Chairman of the City School Board, Community Chest Board (now United Fund), Colleges for Oregon's Future Committee, Co-chairman Radio Free Europe, Agri-businessman of the Year. He was active in establishing a YMCA and donated downtown land for a site. He generously helped to establish Presbyterian Community Hospital, now Merle West Medical Center. Both Andy and his wife Georgia were lifelong members and generous supporters of the Presbyterian

153

CATTLEMAN BUYS FFA SHEEP—A long-time supporter of the Rotary Club sponsored livestock show, Collier stands with purchase.

Church. Along with his brother, Cap, land was donated for the beautiful Collier State Park.

What kind of a person was this man, this captain of industry, this leader of people? Five feet six inches tall, soft-spoken, Andy was not an orator, he used few words trying to express ideas rather than trying to impress people. He possessed what is called the "common touch," a natural sense of equality and humility. He loved to be outdoors, hunted deer, fished at Diamond Lake and in streams. He was a joyful person who loved to ride horseback and play with his grandchildren.

Two events took place which can help to understand this person who did so much for the State and Klamath County. The first happened many years ago. As a youngster, he learned on their farm near Eugene, to whistle in imitation of bird calls. He was an expert whistler by the time he came to Klamath Falls. Here, he assisted in the country dances held at Teeter's Landing warehouse by whistling to the accompaniment of the fiddler. He could whistle remarkably well while on our hike in 1968.

The second event which describes his character occurred in the 1930's. When Willis Mahoney, an ardent Democrat and "new leader," took office as mayor of Klamath Falls, he found the city in bad financial straits. Taxes were not being paid, city bonds were near default and money was not sufficient to run the city. Willis Mahoney was smart. He called in three "rock-ribbed" conservative Republicans to work out a plan to avert a crisis and payoff the debts. These men were: Andy Collier, Tom Watters and Merle West. Their willingness to assist a former antagonist demonstrates clearly that public concern and forgiveness overrode any political pettiness or antagonism generated in the campaign.

C.A. Henderson
Scientist - Educator

The year 1943- The United States is at war. It is October and yet the harvest of the Klamath Basin's potatoes is behind schedule. The machine for the bulk harvesting of potatoes has not yet been invented. The potatoes must be hand picked into sacks. Labor is so scarce the county schools have been let out but there is still danger of the loss of a crop badly needed in the war effort. A dehydrating plant in Klamath Falls is supplying dehydrated potatoes directly to the armed forces.

Arrangements have been made by the Klamath County Extension Service to bring in army men to help in the harvest. The soldiers are to be quartered in the Henley school gymnasium. A mess tent is set up behind the school. The principal's office is to be the dispatch office for the army men. My job is to allocate and dispatch soldiers when the potato growers call for them. This is my first official work with C.A. Henderson.

The men in uniform have just returned from duty in constructing the Alcan Highway through Canada. Some of the officers hate each other. Virtually everyone hates the mess sergeant. For nearly a week when they were in Canada, they had nothing to eat but canned beets. Some of the GI's buy steaks and cook them for themselves.

The farmers treated the men well, fed them well and most paid them though they had not been required to pay wages. Though cold, the weather remained tolerable into November and the crop was saved. The project was a success. This was an example of one of the more unusual services of the county extension agent, C.A. Henderson.

When Charlie Henderson, graduate of Oregon Agricultural College, came to the Klamath country as County Extension agent in 1922, the scene was anything but inviting.

The altitude of most farm land in the Klamath basin is about 4,000 feet. This means a short growing season with the danger of late frost or early frost in the fall. This condition puts severe restrictions on the different varieties of crops that can be profitably grown. Klamath's earliest settlers grew livestock mostly dependent on native wild hay.

Horses provided most farm energy. The single furrow plow called a "foot burner" was the standard implement for tillage. Naturally the size of farms was limited to the amount a farmer could till and plant before it was too late in the season. Eighty acres was considered a farm unit.

The early day farmer was also different from those of today. The radio had only recently been invented. Communication was poor. Many mistrusted college learning. Most grew up on a farm and didn't want anyone telling them how to run their business. If they planted by the moon, they wanted to continue. Mistrust of commercial fertilizer was not uncommon as animal manure had provided the principal fertilizer.

The new agent's first and most difficult problem was one of human relations- getting the attention and cooperation of the farmer. Next came the educational programs. He encouraged milk testing for dairymen to see if they had "star boarders"- cows that gave milk but with little cream. My wife, Marjorie, came into the extension service orbit through 4-H club dairy record work.

Through Henderson's effort, certified potato seed was brought in from Idaho and distributed to a few careful farmers in Klamath County. Bulletins on potato disease were distributed and marketing grades were developed to make the potatoes saleable. This was a tough program to sell farmers. If you grow potatoes, you don't want to throw them away. So you budget for an assistant to teach farmers about diseases, marketing and tillage. Walt Jendrzejewski served Charlie well as an assistant.

In 1932 the 4-H program was a poorly conducted arm led mostly by county school teachers. Charlie brought in Cliff Jenkins to establish a strong corps of independent leaders with dedication and esprit de corps. Their planning and leadership has continued ever since.

ARGRICULTURAL SCIENTIST —In his favorite activity, Charlie Henderson examines potatoes grown for certified seed by Joe Steele on the Howe place near Henley.

How do you get people really interested in improving the quality and profit from animal production? By people contact, of course, as well as by the advice of experts and the result of scientific research. A remarkable job was done in Klamath with the stimulus of a couple of men, L.A. West, a farmer and Tom Watters, a businessman. The Rotary Club was enlisted to sponsor a livestock show, sale and barbeque. It gave the 4-H livestock club members a climax for their year's work. It has given Rotarians a cause that kept the club dedicated to their purpose, "service above self."

Clearly, the work of the extension agent involved many facets: science, banking, political effort, education, but principally in working with people and enlisting their support. C.A. Henderson was a master in directing and persuading people.

In thirty years of school district duty I worked with Elizabeth Henderson, wife of Charlie, who was a music supervisor. During this time both were highly effective in their field but I cannot recall a single instance where one tried to influence the other.

The value of Klamath's extension agent had long been realized by Klamath farmers but the apex of Charlie's long career came with state and national recognition. This is best described in an editorial in the Herald-News dated September 25, 1960:

EDUCATION HEADS HONOR HENDERSON—At the head table in Portland, Elizabeth Henderson sits between Dr. A. L. Strand, president of Oregon State University (on her right) and John Richards, Chancellor of the Oregon System of Higher Education.

"The results of Charlie's activities have been one of the most instrumental factors in raising the economy of the Basin area from one dependent upon cattle, sheep and hay operations to one diversified with a number of crops.

"It was 1922, when he came to Klamath County as Extension Agent.

"The area's agricultural wealth was accounted for by those three things, cattle, sheep and hay.

"The reappraisal was made of the county's farming, recognizing the need for a cash crop of higher value than hay.

"Charlie planted and harvested some test plots of potatoes in late 1922, and the next year half a dozen farmers were encouraged to plant potatoes.

A carload of seed potatoes was obtained and distributed to 44 growers. From that modest start came the tremendous potato industry that is so vital a segment of our agricultural economy.

"In 1923, he promoted founding of the Klamath Dairymen's Association. The group tackled the task of tuberculosis in dairy cattle. Charlie helped organize a herd improvement project, and imported 112 head of high grade and purebred dairy stock for farmers.

"Also, 1923 saw the start of the planting of Hannchen malting barley when Charlie secured a ton and half of seed for use by six growers.

"He encouraged the development of a seed industry.

"All the while, Charlie was leading the fight against crop insects, weeds and other menacing factors.

"His 38 years in the Klamath Basin have all been years of progress, constant growth and unceasing search for even new crops, new ways to strengthen and add to the Basin's agricultural economy.

"June 14, 1955, the Klamath County Chamber of Commerce sponsored "Charlie Henderson Day" and honored him for 33 years of dedicated service.

"On May 21, 1957, he was selected to receive a Superior Service Award from the U.S. Department of Agriculture.

"That citation read, "For outstanding success in helping farmers change a ranch-type of agriculture into a diversified crop area, increasing family income and bringing constructive changes in rural life."

"And if these honors were not sufficient, he has only to look at the living testimonial to his foresight and courage in the form of an ever expanding agricultural economy.

"Few men wear their honors well but, here again, Charlie is an exception.

"In his recent acceptance speech, he said, "This award is not mine alone. Rather, it is something for the entire extension group in

158

the state. Also, this honor should go to the farmers and homemakers of Klamath County for trying out our ideas and suggestions, even at times when they were convinced our ideas were wrong.

Governor Hatfield presents award to Charlie Henderson in September 1960.

Alfred Collier - The Dedicated Citizen

The south suburban area of Klamath Falls, known then as Altamont, was growing rapidly in the early 1930's. The old Altamont School (since burned) had been enlarged and still growth exceeded capacity. In 1933 a wooden building was added to the old Summers School to contain a shop and a home economics room. Together with the old brick building, it was to be called the Altamont Junior High School and to house all seventh and eighth grade pupils from Midland and the south suburbs.

My assignment was, in addition to other duties, to teach wood shop. With some kindly and quick advice from LeRoy Erdman, the Fremont School shop teacher, I assumed the new duty with more courage than expertise. One part of the job was to purchase lumber and materials for the school shop.

I had good reason to enter Swan Lake Moulding Company with a great deal of humility. My purse was small and my knowledge matched my purse. Here I was greeted by a big genial man who treated me as well as though I were a big contractor planning a housing development. This man was Alfred Collier known to his friends as "Cap." Cap's kindness was extended on future buying trips even though only a few boards and nails made my orders as much a nuisance as a profitable transaction. My humility would have been even greater had I known the past accomplishments and future work of this remarkable man.

Alfred D. Collier was born in Eugene, Oregon, on December 14, 1892. There were five boys and one girl in the family. All graduated from the University of Oregon, Alfred in 1914. As a civil engineer, he came to Klamath County in that year to do engineering on the Caledonia and Wocus Marshes. A part of these properties is now known as the Running Y Ranch.

Serving later as deputy county surveyor, Collier engineered the construction of roads, bridges and laid out maps, some of which are still in use.

World War I interrupted his Klamath County career. Upon his return from France, he was married to Ethel Foster, an accountant in the registrar's office at the University of Oregon. The newlyweds picked Klamath County as their home in 1919.

After looking for business opportunities, they purchased a site for a small sawmill on the northwest side of the Swan Lake Valley in connection with a man named Stevenson. From this location came the name Swan Lake Lumber. Cap said that the price of lumber was really low in 1921 but they continued operating, hauling the boards across the north end of Swan Lake Valley with four-horse teams pulling two

SONS OF CHARLES AND JANET COLLIER—Ethan, Percy, Andrew, Alfred and Charles. Alfred (Cap) here appears to be a bit disconsolate, possibly it was because he was the one required to wear the family crocheted lace collar.

loaded wagons. It was two miles across the dry lake bed to a spur of the O.C. and E. railroad. From here, a part of the lumber was transshipped to Wisconsin to a door factory. Lesser grades went into box lumber in Klamath Falls.

After available logs ran out at Swan Lake, the mill was closed and a moulding plant was opened on the railroad at South Sixth Street in 1923 where the business has remained since. One carload of extra wide moulding from this plant was shipped to use in remodeling the White House in Washington, D.C.

Cap Collier was successful in his business enterprises and in the field of finance where he was one of the founding members of First Federal Savings and Loan Association.

If these were his only accomplishments, this story would not be printed here. During the same time his economic work was being carried on, a remarkable record of public service was achieved. As an active American Legionnaire, he served on the committee to build the veteran's memorial building. In 1929 he organized and managed the Legion American Indian Congress. This was held at the fairgrounds where over 1200 Indians from six different tribes met for a celebration and conference.

In further efforts to help veterans, Collier served on the committee that persuaded the Bureau of Reclamation to reduce the cost of homestead land from $90 per acre to $60 per acre and also to refund monies which had accrued through federal leases. On another committee, a low power rate was negotiated with the power company for pumping charges on the Tule Lake Project.

At the time that Collier was appointed to the County Budget Committee in 1933, the county was saddled not only with bonded indebtedness, but with outstanding warrants which were worth less than face value. During his continued service on the committee until 1958, the debt was retired and enough money accumulated to build a courthouse addition without bonds or debt.

He sat on the County Board of Equalization when they had six hundred protests from property owners. These were then adjusted so that there were no appeals from the board's decisions.

Highway improvement was another field in which Alfred Collier was active. It is fortunate for Oregon and for Klamath County that Ethan Collier, Alfred's brother, was assistant to Charles Baldock, chief engineer for the State Highway Commission. Such an association provided a source of information and an avenue for input in highway matters. By persuading the Highway Commission to buy part of the Ewauna and Big Lakes Lumber property, they were able to build a viaduct with only one minor crossing of the railroad spur. Also by getting the property owners to give over 75% of the necessary right-of-way, he persuaded them to widen Sixth Street to four lanes from the railroad to the USRS canal. By promoting the Eastside Bypass and Kit Carson Way, the congestion of traffic on Sixth Street was relieved. Lights were installed by Swan Lake Moulding Company along Sixth from Washburn Way to Altamont.

Cap Collier has had a great curiosity about the natural features and archaeology of the Klamath country and also a sense of history. In our conversations he seemed concerned about doing things that would make a lasting contribution to the people.

Of all public service activities, he is likely to be remembered most for his untiring efforts in the establishment and improvement of parks. After his appointment to the State Parks Advisory Committee, he toured the state with Bill Tugman, editor of the Eugene Register Guard. They entreated county governmental bodies to establish county parks, until now nearly every county has at least one such park. Meanwhile, the State Committee urged greater protection of Oregon's beaches. Strangely enough, it was Representative Tom Young of Baker County whose fine legal work brought out a legislative measure which described the ownership and prevented commercial intrusion onto Oregon's beaches.

The Parks Advisory Committee rendered great service by helping Sam Boardman obtain donations of land. They even persuaded an English corporation to donate land that it had owned for one hundred years. This is now called Sam Boardman State Park.

One of the most beautiful places on the Pacific Coast is located at the junction of Williamson River and Spring Creek. It was here that Peter Skene Ogden of the Hudsons Bay Company entered the Klamath Basin in 1826. He camped among the winter pit houses of the Klamath Indians. The depressions left still show where the former residents lived.

When the Klamath Indians were allowed to receive land allotments, the Blair family and Henry Hoover applied for and received this scenic spot as their private holdings. They later sold it to an Indian trader named R. C. Spink who developed a part of it for recreation property. His daughter, Claudia Lorenz, acquired the property by inheritance. When the Collier's, Cap and his brother Andrew, found that the relocation of Highway 97 would pass near the property they purchased it from Claudia and Bill Lorenz in order to donate it for a state park. It has been dedicated to the memory of their parents, Charles Morse Collier and Janet McCornack Collier.

BIG WHEELS—The log suspended beneath the wheels illustrates how large logs could be dragged by the horse-drawn wheel. Lowell Jones, along with Cap Collier, is acting as curator of the Logging Museum.

The Collier Park property has given an outlet for the love these men felt for the Klamath country, also for their sense of history and their knowledge of the development of the timber industry. A logging museum, the nation's largest and most complete, has been built on the site. It tells the story of lumbering and timber and in Cap's words, "shows them what the industry has done for the United States and why they should support it instead of crucifying it." He has bought, begged, cajoled and urged others to make donations of machines, money, buildings and labor until a complete history of the logging and lumbering industry is shown. Again in Cap's words, "It tells the story of the evolution of the logging industry and its equipment. It challenges the present day to do as much with its greatly improved machines as the old timers did by brute strength and awkwardness."

Thousands of tourists visit the free museum and park each year. Hundreds of local residents utilize the picnic area. Fisherman and boaters can enjoy the 38 degree water which flows evenly all twelve months of the year with enough water "to provide each man, woman and child in the United States with one gallon." For one who wanted to do things with a permanent value, we can think of no greater legacy.

HORSE-DRAWN WATER WAGON—This old horse-drawn water wagon sits in front of the Collier Park Logging Museum. Here, a complete history of the logging and sawmill industry can be seen. Even old cabins and buildings have been moved to the site to make it the most complete logging and lumbering museum in the world.

ED GEARY
GRASSMAN - STATESMAN

Ed Geary was a lousy politician. That may seem to be an unkind thing to say about the man who defended my fiscal policies when I was school superintendent then later persuaded me to run for the state legislature. I'm sure Ed would agree with it.

It may seem strange that the roots of the Geary family and my own go back to the same place, the old Linn County town of Brownsville, Oregon. There on the window of the ageing Presbyterian Church can be seen the name of Edward R. Geary, one of the founders. This man, grandfather of Edward A. Geary, was appointed by the Presbyterian Board of Missions to come to the Oregon Territory. Arriving by way of the Isthmus of Panama, he entered mission work in 1851 at Lafayette, one of the territory's more important towns. In addition to preaching, Dr. Geary served as secretary to Joel Palmer, Superintendent of Indian Affairs in the Territory.

He was active in trying to secure a permanent land base for the Kalapuya Indians but was never successful in this. The remnants of this tribe were removed to the Siletz Indian Reservation.

In another effort, he was eminently successful. Moving to Linn County in 1856, he found the settlers of the region successful in the raising of sheep, but they had no market for the wool. In 1859, representing a group in Brownsville, he traveled to Boston to purchase machinery for a woolen mill. This factory was powered by water from the Calapooia River and was operated by different management over a period of many years.

While the family was living in Brownsville, a son, Edward Payson Geary, was born (Ed's father). He become a doctor and was appointed assistant surgeon for the Oregon-California Railroad. He traveled the right-of-way where the cities of Medford and Grants Pass are now located.

In addition to a distinquished career in medicine, Dr. Geary served as Medford's second mayor and he was also on the Medford School Board.

It was on June 16,1892 in Medford that Edward A. Geary was born. The family moved to Portland in 1898 where Dr. Geary continued a remarkable innovative and successful career.

Meanwhile, young Ed attended the Couch Grade School, Portland Academy, University of Oregon for two years and Wisconsin University for one year. He graduated from Oregon State College in agriculture in 1915. After graduation, he entered the orchard business in Jackson County. He joined the army as a private in 1917. He trained as a balloon observer for the artillery and ended as a sec-

ED GEARY · BALLOONIST—
Smokey Bear hats were common Doughboy issue in World War I. Cloth overseas caps were worn in combat as they would fit under helmets.

(Courtesy of Alice Geary Killiam)

ond lieutenant in the 56th Balloon Company when discharged after the end of World War 1.

There were four sons born to Agnes McCornack Geary and Dr. Edward Payson Geary. Besides Ed, there was Everett, an engineer; Roland, a banker; and Arthur, a lawyer. The McCornack relationship became extremely important as it affected the careers of the four brothers. When the estate of an uncle, E. P. McCornack, was settled they chose land adjacent to Upper Klamath Lake known then as Wocas Marsh and Caledonia Marsh. A part of the land had already been diked off by E.P. McCornack and George Stevenson, another nephew. At this point in development, the only canals into the area had been dug for the purpose of towing logs by steamboat. The logs were cut on the adjacent hills and rafted down to serve the sawmills of Klamath Falls.

In 1917 the process of laying out the canals and laterals to serve the area began. It would still be several years before the land to Wocas Marsh could be drained and the difficult and sometimes heartbreaking process of making it economically sustainable.

Ed Geary became the ranch manager. Martha Geary Smith told

DRAINAGE PUMP—A big gasoline engine attached to a pump is used to drain water from the Caledonia Marsh in 1923. Ed rode horseback to service the pumps.

(Courtesy of Alice Geary K   m)

me that at first they grew only rye and rented pasture to sheep owners. As the enormous area became under better control, a greater diversity of crops was tried. She said that Ed was always experimenting and studying crops that might thrive on the unique soil and water conditions.

In the year 1919, Ed worte to his brother, "We are saving twenty acres of plowed ground for potatoes." Certainly a pioneering effort with this crop. About 1923, purebred cattle were bought from Buck Williams of the Yamsay Ranch to take advantage of the abundant pasture. It was also in that year that a good road development built a dike across the northeast end of Wocas Bay making possible the installation of drainage pumps. Drainage of the marsh produced much more crop land from what formerly had been suitable only for pasture. The operations became so expensive that banker Roland organized a corporation of outside stockholders in Portland to finance the improvements. Alsike clover became a profitable crop; beets also were tried.

The real success story came from the growing of grass seeds. Different varieties were tried. The marketing was led by brother Roland. Geary Brothers bent grass seed was sold all over the world. After five years, the outside stockholders were paid off.

Cattle production was a natural crop to utilize the green pasture after the seed harvest. The grass straw was very nutritive especially when mixed with molasses.

The production of small grass seed, such as alsike clover and grass, required pioneering efforts and the invention, as well as manufacture, of new machinery. Giant buckrakes and later covered transport wagons were used to handle the light and elusive seed.

167

CALEDONIA MARSH—Grain grows where only tules could thrive. This was the first part of the reclamation project. Note the wide wheels for the soft land.

Storage of the grass straw presented a different problem than storing hay. The harvesting operation had to be carried out at exactly the right time to prevent maturity or weather from destroying the crop. Martha Smith said that "sometimes as many as ninety men might be on the payroll."

What kind of a person was Ed Geary? My first contact with him was when we successfully asked him to donate grass seed for the Henley High School football field. Next, in 1949 I was pushing a conservation program and had heard of Ed's efforts in protecting hawks and owls. We persuaded him to help in this program.

By 1961, as a chamber of commerce director in charge of the tax committee, I asked him to attend a public meeting on taxation. At this point, my image of Ed Geary was that of a wealthy, articulate and socially active person · carefree and independent. His attractive wife, Marian, was active in promoting better juvenile programs and care for delinquents.

Where was the real Ed Geary? His daughter, Alice, told me that he was a kind and loving father but she always wondered why they couldn't travel around on Sundays like other people. Her father always had to work. His brothers worried about his health at one point in his life as they thought that he was overworked. Sister-in-law Martha said regardless of circumstances, company or commitments, Ed Geary went to bed at nine o'clock.

The heavy burden of farm management did not prevent Geary from serving the industry on the State Board of Agriculture. He was first appointed by Governor Martin, then reappointed by Governor Sprague. He again was reappointed and served as chairman of this important body under Governor Snell.

Geary was first elected to the Oregon State Legislature in 1951. His intelligence and integrity were quickly recognized by his colleagues and in 1955 he became the Speaker of the House. With his downstate support and Portland connections, he became a very powerful legislator. He was on friendly terms with Governor Paul Patterson and Senate President Elmo Smith. With Henry Semon by his side and Harry Boivin in the Senate, they brought off much legislation favorable to Klamath County.

Who said Ed Geary was a lousy politician? After his long career in agricultural development, he could not see anything except realistic solutions to problems. He met every issue head-on. In a few minutes anyone knew where he stood on issues.

Oregon had two great problems in 1955: insufficient state revenue to carry the programs and a deteriorating highway system that had to be saved. School populations were growing and costs going up with a resulting increase in property taxes.

ED GEARY · SPEAKER—At the apex of his career, Geary was one of the most influential men in Oregon.

(Courtesy of Alice Geary Killiam)

A tax expert and a realist, Geary knew a sales tax would not pass an Oregon referral so a sizeable increase in state income tax was passed for general fund purposes. The highway problem was also met head-on. Geary felt that large trucks were not paying a proportionate share of highway costs. At that point, very little research had been done on damage from trucks. Along with Elmo Smith a weight-mile tax was proposed. Since Oregon was one of the first states to pioneer such a tax, the trucking industry was incensed. They immediately raised money for a referral which delayed the collection of the tax until after the election on the referral.

Governor Paul Patterson died in office, Senate President Elmo Smith succeeded him. Smith ran for governor to succeed himself and I think Geary knew he was committing political suicide in running against Boivin. Robert Holmes and the Democrats ran on a program of income tax reductions. Elmo Smith and Geary were defeated.

Only seven Republicans of the sixty in the House of Representatives survived the landslide. But the weight-mile tax on trucks was passed.

Geary visited me occasionally in the legislature after his retirement from the farm. He bore no resentment over his defeat and was always supportive and encouraging in his attitude.

Like I said, Ed Geary was a lousy politician but he left a legacy of solid accomplishments for Klamath County: a sound method of highway finance and a tax system to support state government that lasted until they started using state funds to pay people's rent and property tax.

NELSON REED AND THE
KLAMATH RIVER COMPACT

Pittsburgh, Pennsylvania, is so far from Klamath County that it seems a most unlikely source for a tourist. Alfred Reed, editor of the Pittsburgh Gazette however, was such a tourist. His summer visits in the early 1900's to the old Eagle Ridge Tavern on Upper Klamath Lake led to a series of events having a decided impact on the Klamath country.

Reed first came for the sport fishing on the lake. Then, hearing that Averill Harriman was going to bring a railroad through Klamath Falls, he decided to buy two lots there for investment. One was at sixth and Klamath Avenue, the other on twelfth and Klamath. Nelson Reed, son of Alfred, came along on these visits and fell in love with the Klamath country. No person, not even his wife, Margaret, will ever fully know of his contributions to the Klamath region.

Nelson Reed was born on June 21, 1895 in Pittsburgh where he went through grade eight in public school. After attending a private prep school, he graduated from Princeton University. His attendance at Harvard Law School was cut short when his vision problems forced him to quit. I have the feeling this legal training, though incomplete, must have made a contribution to his later skill in dealing with the legal professionals.

As World War 1 approached he was admitted to officer's training school in New York but he was dismissed because of vision problems. After trying unsuccessfully to enlist in every branch of the service, wouldn't you know he was drafted and received an unusual quick promotion even before receiving his uniform. The newly inducted recruits were gathering at the railroad station for departure. As they celebrated their new status over half were drunk. Nelson was approached by a worried officer who said, "You are sober so I'm promoting you to corporal." After training he arrived in France where he was later made an officer in the artillery.

Following the Armistice, he returned to Pittsburgh and in 1923 brought his new bride, a Vassar graduate, to visit the Klamath country. They first camped at Harriman Resort where she hated the mosquitoes and the food. She liked it little better when they moved camp to the Eagle Ridge Tavern area.

Despite his wife's protests, Reed decided to live in Klamath and went into the sawmill business on a site back of the hills beyond the old OTI campus. After four years he gave up when the banks would no longer loan money. It was a dismal and discouraging time for the Reeds. When I later became acquainted with him, I thought he was kidding me when he told me of his job poisoning grasshoppers on the

LT. NELSON REED 1917—
Rejected from law school
and officer's training school,
because of his vision, Nelson
was found to be just right for
a draftee. In the Artillery, he
worked his way up to become
an officer.

EAGLE RIDGE TAVERN—A popular place that could be reached by boat. It attracted tourists from the East including the Reeds.

Klamath Marsh in the 1930's.

In 1936 Nelson Reed was appointed as head of the newly organized Employment Service. He had one employee and an office in the post office. His work led him into acquaintance with the contractors who were building the road around Crater Lake National Park. Nelson must have served them well as when he later raised the money and purchased the Caterpillar tractor agency, they returned to buy equipment for him. Prosperity returned to the Reed family and never departed. The equipment business was sold after thirteen years of operation.

In retirement both husband and wife enjoyed outstanding success in investment and resource management.

It is hard to describe personal qualities and activities of Nelson Reed without bordering on exaggeration. He was essentially a modest person but his abilities and integrity were so well known and appreciated by community leaders that they proposed and pushed him to accept public service jobs which offered little or no renumeration.

If failure did not discourage or humiliate Reed, financial success did not change him from being a public spirited, active, exuberant outdoor guy. He was such an expert trap shooter that his wife complained about the numerous trophies "made like little silver men carrying guns." She finally persuaded him to encourage trophies such as silver dishes.

Although an expert fisherman, he did not hunt deer. During duck and upland bird seasons, Mrs. Reed complained, "There never is heard a sensible word."

Nelson loved the Klamath country so wrote a book of poems about it called "Tule Smoke." After publishing it he gave the book to the Klamath County Museum to sell to help them raise money. His talent as a writer also blossomed each New Year's holiday at the Rotary Club when he donned the robes and makeup of an oriental prophet, Dr. Who. In this guise he joyfully and mercilessly castigated and berated the town's leading citizens through his prophecy.

The Reeds in retirement often were world travelers and generously provided slide programs for service organizations.

He ran in 1934 unsuccessfully against the famous Willis Mahoney for mayor of Klamath Falls. He served two terms on the Klamath Union High School Board. When the new County Library was to be built, he was appointed chairman of the committee to select a suitable location. When he was elected city councilman, he quit saying that he couldn't get anything done.

One of the most significant events in the economic development of the Klamath Country has been the granting and settlement of the homesteads in the Tule Lake Basin. The waters of Lost River were diverted into the Klamath River. Tule Lake receded uncovering thousands of acres of fertile and productive soil. Nearly all of the lake bed south of the California stateline was property of the U.S. Government. Much of it has been reclaimed for bird refuge and water control but other sections have been put to farm use. Some farm lands have been leased but following World War One the first homesteads were opened there for the war veterans.

Later another section was prepared and sold to qualified veterans. Following World War Two the third part of the big lake bed was set aside to be granted by drawing to veterans who met and qualified as farmers.

Sam Wynn, Bob Norris and Nelson Reed were selected to prepare and supervise this operation. As usual, Reed was picked as chairman. Veterans from all over the United States gathered to witness and participate in the event which was carried off successfully on Dec. 1946. Over the years the process has created a community made up principally of war veterans.

If Nelson Reed had performed no other public service, his work in one capacity would cause him to go down in history as a great benefactor of the Klamath country including Northern California. This event was the passage and adoption of the Klamath River Compact. It is best described in his own words: "Not since the rains came and Old Man Noah built the Ark has there been so much talk about water as in the past few years. Most of you have read about the squabbles in the California Legislature all last session about water. While the problem has not been so acute in Oregon nevertheless we think that we are very fortunate to have been able to get our Klamath River Compact passed by both Oregon and California last winter and approved by the Congress this summer.

"Some of you may remember that about eight years ago the U.S. Engineers held a meeting in Klamath Falls at which they discussed the possibility of diverting the Klamath River into the Pitt River and thence into the Sacramento and the big California Valleys. In fact, the U.S. Engineers went so far as to make a preliminary survey of that scheme. At that time some of our more far sighted citizens formed the Land Use Committee and began to think how they could protect our water. Some of you may say "Well if we couldn't use the water at that time, why not let California have it?" It is basic water law that whoever first puts water to beneficial use establishes a right to that water. Therefore, if California diverted the Klamath River and used it to irrigate in the Sacramento Valley, they would acquire a right to that water. In later years if we needed that water we could not get it back. It would be California's forever.

"With that threat in mind the land Use Committee urged our Legislators of that time, Ed Geary and Hank Semon to see what they could do. They persuaded the 52nd Oregon Legislature to appropriate $25,000 to create the Klamath River Commission to make a

GEORGE STEVENSON—As an engineer his service was valuable in explaining to congress the Klamath River problem. He donated the property for Stevenson park on Lost River.

JIM KERNS—Since serving on the Klamath River Compact Commission, Jim Kerns has been a strong and well informed advocate of increasing the upstream storage capacity of the Klamath watershed. He has persistently approached governors, federal officials and the public in pursuit of this valuable resource development.

survey of the water and land resources of the Upper Klamath Basin, and attempt to workout an interstate compact with a similar commission in California for the equitable apportionment of our water and a system of priorities for its use. Governor Patterson then appointed George Stevenson, Harry Pearson, Jim Kerns, Jr., Ralph Koozer of Ashland and myself to be the Oregon Klamath River Commission. I became Chairman. To make a survey of water resources we hired Lewis Stanley whom some of you have met. Stanley spent about a year studying all the available reports of the Bureau of Reclamation, Copco, The Soil Conservations Service, the State Engineers Office, and others. The California Commission was making a similar survey both in California and Oregon at the same time. Our report was published and submitted to the Oregon Legislature in the winter of 1953-54.

"You may remember that about that time the report of the Bureau of Reclamation came out. They had two proposals for increasing or guaranteeing more storage in the Upper Klamath Lake that we did not like. One was a system of very expensive dikes to raise the level of the lake that would involve flooding out and buying already highly productive land in order to irrigate potentially productive land. The other was to dredge a deep channel in the lake so the water could be drawn way down in low water years if need be. It would have resulted in very ob-

175

UPPER KLAMATH LAKE—The lake, Oregon's largest, provides a great reservoir allow-
ing an even flow of water into the state of California. It has great value for wildlife,

jectionable mud flats. Their other proposition that we particularly objected to was to divert the Klamath River near Keno, pumping it up onto Butte Valley and dropping it off Ikes Mountain through a power
plant, the profits from the power thus generated to pay for the irrigation costs in Butte Valley. That scheme would have barred the present
Copco development at Big Bend which will eventually result in a very
substantial tax revenue to Klamath County and Oregon and will furnish much needed power for more industry such as the Johns-
Manville plant in Klamath County.

"We had held only a few meetings with the California Klamath
River Commission when both Commissions came to the conclusion
that there were about 300,000 acres of land in the Upper Klamath
Basin not presently irrigated that could be irrigated in the future;
200,000 of these were in Oregon and 100,000 in California. We further agreed that there was sufficient water to irrigate this much new
land if water for power was subordinated to water for irrigation. We
agreed also that if additional storage facilities were created to save the
spring runoff that is now wasted down the river each year, there would
be sufficient water for both irrigation and power development, not only
for the present but for the foreseeable future. We therefore agreed
that we should consider the Upper Klamath Basin as one unit and
disregard state lines in our Compact.

"After a number of meetings with the California Commission we

recreation and irrigation. As its waters rush through the steep canyon through the Cascade Mountains, power is generated for use in both states.

agreed on a rough draft of our Compact. We thereupon sent copies of it to the various state and federal bodies that were interested, and asked for their comments. In general we got very skimpy replies, particularly from the Department of Interior who in effect said "we'll think it over but we don't think much of it. Washington will let you know." We then held a number of public meetings in Oregon and California and asked for comments. Apparently most of our local people agreed for only a few showed up at the meetings and very few objected when it was explained what we were trying to do.

   "About this time Copco was negotiating with the Department of Interior for the renewal for 50 years of the Contract for control of the Link River Dam and the use of the Upper Klamath Lake for storage. Copco was willing to agree with the Bureau of Reclamation and Department of Interior to subordinate water for power to water for irrigation on the Klamath Project. Both state Commissions felt that they should also subordinate power to irrigation on off-project lands as well, and we refused to recommend to the Secretary of the Interior that he sign a new contract with Copco unless that was agreed. Copco then agreed to this condition in a contract with the River Commissions in consideration for which the River Commissions agreed that any water diverted from the Klamath River in the Upper Basin should be returned to the river above Keno so it would be available to Copco for power. At the same time we assisted the Water Users Protective Association

NELSON REED—Picture taken about the time he served on the Klamath River Commission.

in obtaining a very favorable off the Klamath project pumping rate, about 7½ mills which is about half the old rate. It will enable land owners outside the Project to farm lands economically that could not otherwise be farmed. Copco has obtained this rate from the PUC in Oregon but is still trying to get it in from the California Utilities Commission.

"To me the sessions with Copco, the Department of Interior, and the two River Commissions were the most interesting of my water experiences. At one meeting in Sacramento we had nine lawyers. When the session was over I remarked that I would like to thank all the lawyers for a fine legal education in water rights and that when I got back to Klamath Falls I hoped they would have no objection if I hung out my shingle as a lawyer without taking any bar exams. One of the California lawyers said, "Why would you want to be a lawyer; you're doing alright." I said, "Oh, I might just want to be a pain in the neck to some guys up home I have always wanted to be a pain in the neck to."

"But seriously, I feel that both the Oregon and California Commissions had some of the finest lawyers you would ever run across. Our Mr. Howard Stinson had been a lawyer for the Bureau of Reclamation for a number of years, and for the past four years had acted as legal consultant for the Columbia River Compact. He was admittedly an outstanding authority on river compacts. California's Mr. Moskowitz was one of the most honest, straight forward, intelligent, fair minded and well informed legal minds that I have met. It was a pleasure to work with those two.

"After Our Oregon survey was completed Lewis Stanley was made State Engineer. I think that our recommendation to Governor Patterson might have had something to do with it. As State Engineer, Lewis was a great help to us, particularly in presenting our Compact to the State Legislature. State Senator Harry Boivin was invaluable to us in Salem. Without his skillful handling of our bill up there it is a question if it would have passed.

"When we couldn't get any definite answers from Washington about our Compact, we made up our minds that we would have to take our brain child to Washington ourselves and try to sell it to the many government bureaus that were interested. And if you don't think there were many, I shall name just a few; The Bureau of the Budget, the Department of Interior, the Forest Service, the Department of Agriculture, the Indian Service, the U.S. Engineers, the Health, Education and Welfare Services, the Bureau of Mines, (don't ask me why), and last but not least the Department of Justice. Without too much trouble we softened up all but the Justice Department. They were inclined to think that Uncle got here first, owned all the water and the states nor anybody else had a right to dabble around in their water.

"When I was out of the country for the first Washington meeting, Big George Stevenson went for Oregon. George, because of his training as an engineer and his experience as an irrigation farmer, was an invaluable man to the Oregon Commission. Later I attended two sessions in Washington. Dealing with Washington bureaus is very frustrating as any of you know who have been there. Time and expense mean nothing to the bureaucrats. Without batting an eye after they have had a year to study your proposal, they come back sometime later and say, "Our lawyers haven't had time to really study it yet." Sometimes we wondered if they had even read it.

"At our last meeting in Washington I was afraid that we were sunk. The Justice Department was still putting us off and not giving us any definite answer. Then all of a sudden, they offered their own proposal instead of the clauses they were objecting to in the Compact, and we accepted them delightedly. Honestly it would have taken a smart lawyer to tell them from our own. In fact several smart lawyers said there was no difference.

"As the Compact never got to Congress till the closing days of the session when they were fighting bitterly about Hell's Canyon and segregation, I thought again we were sunk. But thanks to Bert Phillips, Chairman of the California Commission, who is a cross between an airedale and a bulldog when it comes to fighting congressional committees, and assisted by Jim Stearns of Tule Lake, who is no mean battler himself, they got the compact passed. Congressman Engel of California and Senator Kuckel of California, of course, had the influence we needed. Without California's power we never would have made it in Washington.

"Basically the Compact nails down for all time the waters of the Upper Klamath Basin are for our own use. It gives priority to water for domestic irrigation use over power not only at present but in the future as well. In other words an application for a water right to irrigate filed twenty years from now will take precedence over a filing for power or other use that is filed today. It says that there shall be no diversion of the Klamath River from the Upper Basin to California unless it will be returned to the Klamath River above Keno. It says that Oregon shall be granted sufficient water to irrigate an additional 200,000 acres and that California shall be granted sufficient water to irrigate 100,000 acres. No amount of water per acre is specified. It provides for a permanent three man Commission to carry out the terms of the Compact. The Commissions shall consist of the State Engineer of Oregon, the head of the Water Resources Department of California and a Federal Representative.

"We believe that the Compact is a fine thing for this community. It will protect our water against diversion and guarantee us a chance to develop our water resource fully over a period of time as it becomes economically profitable to do so. The four years I spent working on the Compact have been the most interesting of any non-paying job I ever had. And now, I am going to brag a bit. We got the job done and turned back about ten thousand dollars of our appropriation to the General fund. I hope that won't cause the Governor to call another special session. I thank you."

Nelson Reed died in November 1970. It was like this humble man to request that no service be held to honor his passing. His work should not be forgotten. If the blue herons still have a place to wade, and the spoonbills can go about their upside-down search for plankton after one hundred years have passed, it will probably be due to the work of Nelson Reed and others on the Klamath River Compact Commission who drew the River Agreement.

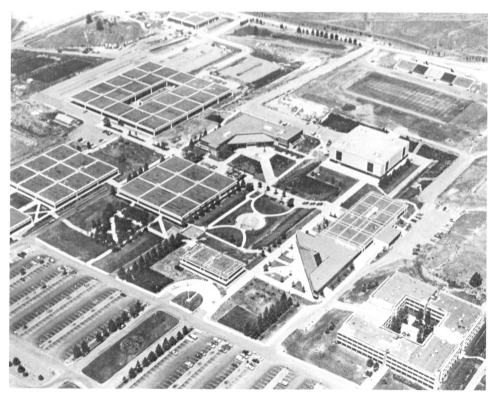

OREGON INSTITUTE OF TECHNOLOGY—Additions have been made to campus buildings since the big move. Advanced programs in medical technology and electronics have been expanded.

(Courtesy of O.I.T.)

The Year OTI Came off the Hill

The scene: Outer office of Oregon Senate President Ben Musa. Time: Late spring 1963. Characters: Senator Harry Boivin, Representative George Flitcraft and I (Rep. Carrol Howe). In our hands a copy of the Klamath paper- Herald and News. It carried big headlines. Winston Purvine had announced that the legislative Ways and Means Committee approved funds for the new buildings and campus for OTI with construction virtually assured.

Was our meeting in Musa's office a joyful one? Not so! The article did not mention a few little things to be taken care of before the money would become available. First, House Bill 2105 would have to receive a majority in the 60 member House of Representatives. Then it must pass the Senate, after which the Governor, Mark Hatfield would have to sign it.

The opponents of the bill were formidable. The State Board of Higher Education was against it. The Chancellor and the OTI President Winston Purvine opposed it. It was especially opposed by the heads of other higher education institutions in Oregon who wanted part of the money.

BOIVIN AS GOVERNOR—Senator Boivin was twice elected President of the Senate. This picture taken in 1965 shows him serving as governor when Mark Hatfield was out of the state. Boivin always got along well with Hatfield but one Senate President, serving while the Governor was out of the state, pardoned a life term murderer.

The State Board, Chancellor and Purvine wanted the school to be moved off the hill and into the new campus over a period of years allowing for a split campus and more orderly transition. The three Klamath legislators knew that the future of the school would be in great jeopardy if the funds were not approved in the 1963 legislative session. We also knew that there were only three of the 90 legislators who were deeply concerned about the future of the school. It is understandable, given the setting and opposition, why the three were less than enthusiastic about the big headlines.

OTI like all other state higher institutions had its beginning with political activity. The people of Klamath led by Vern Owens had embraced the institution and taken support for OTI as a civic duty. Formed as Oregon Vocational School under the State Board of Education, local people felt it would fare better under the State Board of Higher Education. Influential legislators from Klamath were able to bring about the transfer even though the State Board wanted to retain jurisdiction and the Higher Board welcomed it about like a hungry family would welcome adopting a poverty-stricken relative.

The 1961 Legislature was not favorably impressed with OTI when they made their visit. It was housed in the old wooden marine barracks where the heating and maintenance costs were excessive.

They were also critical of operations. A cutback in enrollment and course offerings was ordered.

Faced with such overwhelming odds against the school, what forces and factors could bring about passage of the big appropriation? For one thing- community effort. The Chamber of Commerce entertained both Ways and Means Committee members and the Board of Higher Education in 1961. Flitcraft and I recall going duck hunting with House Speaker Robert Duncan at the invitation of Dick Henzel. Local people raised money through donations to purchase the property from the O'Connors for the present site of the school. By 1963, we were able to promise geothermal heat and substantially reduced maintenance costs.

I give much of the credit for passage of the entire construction and appropriation to Senator Boivin. Although each of the Klamath delegation had personal assets in the bank of good will at the legislature, Boivin had the "know how" and friends in the power structure of the assembly. He had been very much involved in founding the so-called coalition of moderate Democrats and Republicans that had controlled the Senate since the election of Boyd Overhulse in 1959. He did not call it a coalition but "a group of responsible Republicans and Democrats."

Another group in which the Klamath delegation was active was call the Jackrabbits. This was led by Boivin and Representative Bob Smith. Their purpose was to keep from losing the representation from Eastern Oregon Counties. The name was derived from an Oregonian article written by a Portland State College professor who stated, that "Eastern Oregon legislators represented very few people but many jackrabbits." The moniker helped give the loosely-knit but loyal organization a rallying point.

Boivin was not a talkative individual and I suspect that few people would know what he was doing unless it was his wife, Vivian, who was an excellent secretary. He might offer me advice but never pressure. We never seemed to disagree on Klamath County problems.

I did not fully realize Harry's influence in legislature until I was confronted in 1963 at a social event by Rep. Sam Wilderman of Portland. He was considered the unofficial lobbyist for Portland State College where his wife worked. His message, "Call off Boivin or there won't be any OTI left." My reply, of course, was that I did not control Senator Boivin.

George Flitcraft, who worked inside Ways and Means Committee, stated it well when he said, "It was late in the session and we did not dare let it be known how much the appropriation meant to us or pressure could be brought to bear that we did not want." George, although a minority party Republican, had a good relationship with

Speaker of the House, Clarence Barton. Barton, from Coos Bay, liked to imagine himself a liberal but actually he was a hard-nosed conservative when dealing with public money. He understood and appreciated Flitcraft's work on Ways and Means Committee.

Our greatest ally on the House side of the legislature was Stafford Hansell of Umatilla County. Although a Republican, he had been appointed by Barton as vice-chairman of the Joint Ways and Means Committee. He was known to be tough, articulate and incorruptible - a formidable opponent. Fortunately he was a fellow Jackrabbit and a good friend of both Flitcraft and me. (If George had been re-elected in 1964, Hansell would have been head of the House and Flitcraft, chairman of the Ways and Means.)

Some other Ways and Means members who served to help the preservation of OTI were Senator Dan Thiel of Astoria, Lynn Newbry of Jackson County, Debbs Potts of Josephine and Ward Cook from Portland. Representative Don McKinnis of Union County, while extremely critical of the institution, was very helpful in passage of the bill.

Hansell understood the factors and forces at work in the legislative assembly better than anyone. In a Klamath Falls speech he said, "Boivin is like a meadowlark. Whenever OTI is mentioned he goes flopping off with a feigned broken wing leaving Howe and Flitcraft to guard the nest." After this the Klamath delegation called House Bill 2105 the "Meadowlark Bill."

Flitcraft worked early and late on Ways and Means Committee evaluating Oregon's needs. He earned the respect of his fellow workers and had no time for the production of press releases and personal publicity. He was narrowly defeated in the 1964 election by a person who ironically was appointed to the teaching staff at OTI after the 1965 session.

It is impossible to assess my own part in the preservation and restructuring of OTI. As a minority party member, I had little power but had influence as an Education Committee member. As a Jackrabbit, Eastern Oregon contacts were no problem. Fortune had smiled upon me in several other ways that led to friendly joint efforts. Since Klamath's school finance problems were the same as those in Portland, I was joined by Senator Jean Lewis in the fight over basic school distribution when we co-sponsored a finance bill. It brought with it the help and lasting friendship of George Baldwin, Business Manager of the Portland School District. It also made available to me the valuable research capacity of that district. While these assets were great, with them came the opposition of the University of Oregon Education Department and others who felt tax equalization was the prime purpose of the state basic school support fund.

A second fortunate occurrence was that Governor Mark Hatfield

STAFFORD HANSELL OF UMATILLA
COUNTY—With unquestioned integrity
and with plenty of guts, Hansell is a good
friend and a tough antagonist. His ability
was so great that democrat Governor
Straub asked him, a conservative
republican, to head his executive department.

FLITCRAFT AND YOUTHFUL
GOVERNOR—Representative
George Flitcraft, as a member
of the Ways and Means Committee, was in an excellent
position to watch and in-
fluence the OTI appropriation.
Governor Mark Hatfield was
so youthful at this time that
his critics called Salem, the
capital city, "Boy's Town."

had asked me to be principal sponsor of his Port of Portland bills. (The Port of Portland is a state agency.) This work brought me into a cooperative relationship with Rep. Ed Whelan, a strong labor man and a real force in the Democrat Party. Whelan later became state head of the A.F.L.-C.I.O.

The weather brought about another lucky but less important incident in my personal relationships. It seldom snows in Salem but on this first day of the session when we returned to our parking space, the windshields were covered with partially frozen snow. An elderly couple behind us were trying without success to remove snow from their windshield. Being a Klamathite, we had a windshield scraper and took the snow from their windshield. It turned out to be Jake Bennett, the curmudgeon of the House of Representatives. He was a former city commissioner in Portland and was an expert "battler." He was both articulate and mean. He so frustrated the Speaker, Barton, that he broke his gavel trying to get Jake to sit down. The windshield incident made a lasting friend of Bennett. I doubt if he ever voted for my bills as he

NEW CAMPUS—Boivin and Howe view campus that resulted from one-shot move from the old Marine Barracks.

didn't vote for any bills but at least he didn't fight me. He did, however, try to get me to quit smoking so that I would live longer.

The Capitol Scene: Late May 1963. Associated Press story written by Paul Harvey is headlined:

Weary Solons Prolong Hate-Wracked Session

He wrote: "Bone weary legislators exhausted by 141 days of hard work, hate each other to an extent that has not been seen in more than a quarter of a century." The Ways and Means Committee is castigated by Hatfield for cutting the budget with a meat cleaver. The Meat Cutter's Union has presented each Ways and Means member a meat cleaver tie clasp. We still have dinner frequently with Staff and Mary Elizabeth Hansell. I never ask him for anything - maybe that's why they like to join us.

The time has arrived. House Bill 2105 has come to the floor with a "do pass." Hansell carries the bill wearing his meat cleaver tie clasp.

Measure No. *HB 2105*

SENATE ROLL CALL

Date ....

	Ex.	Abs	Nay	Aye		Ex.	Abs	Nay	Aye
AHRENS			X		INSKEEP				✓
BOIVIN				✓	IRELAND		X		✓
CHAPMAN				✓	LETH				✓
COOK, VERN				✓	MAHONEY		X		
COOK, WARD				✓	MONAGHAN				✓
CORBETT, ALFRED				✓	NATERLIN				✓
CORBETT, ALICE				✓	NEWBRY	X			
ELFSTROM				✓	OVERHULSE				✓
FADELEY		X			PEARSON				✓
FLEGEL				✓	POTTS	X			
HALLOCK				✓	STADLER				✓
HARE				✓	THIEL				✓
HOPKINS				✓	WILLNER				✓
HUSBAND	X				YTURRI			X	
HUSTON				X	MR. PRESIDENT			X	

TOTALS ▶ 3 | 6 | 2

Message from Boivin, "The meadowlarks can leave the nest now."

LA 19 2R

Rep. John Dellenback of Medford rises to question the language in the bill. He wanted the bill sent back to committee to correct the language. Did someone get him to send it back to kill the bill? John is a good friend of mine, a highly respected attorney. I hesitate to question his legal opinion. My prepared speech remains undelivered. John was sincere and the bill was corrected and came back for a floor vote. Keep your mouth shut, Howe. Let Hansell handle it! The bill passed the House with only three negative votes. Even Jake Bennett voted for it. Hatfield has been a long time friend of OTI. We feel sure that he will sign it if it passes the Senate.

June 3, 1963 A note came from Boivin on a scorecard showing the Senate vote saying, "The meadowlarks can leave the nest now."

I tell my wife: "I will never run against Boivin." Of course, I don't tell him that.

ANGUS BOWMER—Small in stature and pleasant in demeanor. The courage and determination that lay beneath this exterior was well disguised.

ANGUS BOWMER - THE ZEALOT

A double sleeping bag of brown canvas was one of the few luxuries we had allowed ourselves at the time of our marriage. We had also one single air mattress which we placed crosswise in the bag to pad our hips and shoulders. On this occasion we are lying in the bag on the floor of our one bedroom house at Hager siding near Klamath Falls. Sleeping in our bedroom are guests Bob and Audrey Stedman of Medford.

Bob had served as teacher, coach and play director at Henley High School during 1936-38. He was now teacher and dramatics director in the Medford City Schools.

As I lay in my reasonably comfortable sleeping bag, I'm a little restless. First, my wife had been uptight over the danger of one of our ample supply of mice running over us. I did not want her to disturb our guest by screaming in terror. In addition, I was worried about the man sleeping on our davenport in the living room. This man was Angus Bowmer. The Stedmans had brought him over to talk with Fred Peterson, County School Superintendent, about sponsoring Shakesperian plays or playlets in the county schools. They hoped that I might help them to persuade our school superintendent to give financial encouragement to their cultural effort. I felt sorry for the poor guy Bob called Gus. It was in the depression years and I could hardly persuade

Pete (we did not call him this to his face.) to buy curtains for the classrooms let alone for dramatics.

Bowmer was such a nice guy and so enthusiastic that I did not want to tell him that his Shakespeare thing would never go anywhere. I felt there had been too many high school students antagonized by being required to memorize Shakespeare in literature classes.

I worried too because our friends, Audrey and Bob Stedman, seemed caught up in the hair-brained idea that people would go to see a group of amateur actors play Shakespeare. Finally sleep eases my anxiety. My batting average as a prophet has been about the same ever since.

The success of the Shakesperian Festival and other ventures in the field of drama are so well known that little need be said here. How can one account for the almost unbelievable development of the movement from almost nothing to its present status?

One of the most fortunate events in the life of Angus Bowmer occurred when he was selected to be a judge in a contest of one-act plays sponsored by the Oregon State Grange at Phoenix, Oregon. It was here that the young college English and dramatics teacher first observed the stagecraft and production talent of Bob Stedman.

It is 1984, in my home are the people who enjoyed the luxury of our only bed back in 1939, Bob and Audrey Stedman. The following taped interview gives the genesis and roots of the theatre movement in Ashland:

Carrol: How did Gus Bowmer get you into it in the first place?

Bob: Well, I was doing a show for the grange at Phoenix. All the granges had one act plays and they would go together and do shows. Then they were going to pick the best play in Oregon. Gus was one of the people to judge and when he saw me he asked me to come to Southern Oregon. He said, "There are a lot of things that I want to do and I think you can help me."

Bob: I said, "I don't have any money." He told me that if I could only stay one term, he thought he could get some money for me so that's exactly what I did. I got enough money, my twelve dollars for my tuition and I stayed at home. Then Gus gave me a job teaching half of his play production class. He would take half the class upstairs and lecture and I would show them how to build scenery and paint and that kind of thing below.

Carrol: It seems overwhelming that you could get this going without any money. Do you remember what was the first play that you tried?

Bob: Gus knew he wanted to do something but he wasn't quite sure. One day he said to me, "Come over, I want to show you something." So we got in his car and went up on that high drive on the mountain and looked down at the old chautauqua building and he said, "What is

190

PETRUCHIO—It can be seen that hours of work would be required to make a costume for the Shakesperaian character.

that?" I said, "That's a Shakespeare theater." He said, "We're going to have one there one of these days." We didn't have any money and we didn't know just what to do. We went down into the old place and it was raining. It was in March. We sat down and planned and early in 1935 people in Ashland asked us to organize and head the 4th of July celebration. Gus said that we'd do it if they would do it in a little shell for a Shakespeare Festival. With the WPA and all the letters that Mr. Roosevelt had, we got that thing done and immediately started to plan a play. Well, Gus thought that maybe we could do one show in the Normal School and then in the spring we could do a different one when school was over. Then we would do the second one that we did in the spring in the old chautauqua building. But we did the first one at Southern Oregon and then we trooped it over to Klamath. We did Merchant of Venice and started Twelfth Night. So that first Shakesperian Festival in 1935 was two times Twelfth Night and one time Merchant of Venice.

Carrol: In those days everything had to be initiated originally as there was no precedent to go on. What were some of the first critical problems that you came up against?

Bob: The first thing, of course, there was no money and no lights. My problem was to do all the lights and I obtained from the city four, thousand-watt spot floods and I had to use a concentric ring to make the light stay in the area rather than all over the city. That was probably one of the things.

Carrol: As I recall, Audrey, you worked with the first Mrs. Bowmer. What was your main operation to start with?

Audrey: I was the jack-of-all-trades. Whatever needed to be done I did and I did a lot of the costume making. You have to remember that it was right in the depression and there was no money for anything. I think we had forty dollars for a budget and all the costumes were made out of canton flannel which is a heavy-knapped flannel and just whatever we could find. People of the valley opened up and they gave us old bedspreads and draperies, just anything that would make into a costume. Then all the sewing was done by volunteers. They used long underwear for tights for the men. We had old jewelry that we used for decorating, just anything that we could get our hands on, feathers, feather boas and just anything that would make up into a costume. It had to be done from scratch. We had to dye the flannel before making the costumes.

Carrol: Where was your principal workshop?

Audrey: Well, we worked at the theater on the lawn. There was a big sort of courtyard with big trees and we worked out there with extension cords. Everyone had their own machine and took it with them. We worked too at Bowmer's house and at the Normal School. We had quite a few volunteers, I would say around eight. There were usually four.

Carrol: What was Mrs. Lois Bowmer's role in getting this founded?

Audrey: She was a great backbone and as Bob often said, Gus would get the idea and Lois would carry it out. We called her the art director. She designed most of the costumes and cut them out. We would cut patterns and then we would fit them on. She had a hand in everything.

Carrol: Audrey, I was wondering how many years did you work?

Audrey: I worked five years. I started in 1935 and worked up to 1939 when Bob and I were married.

Carrol: Now you were a student at Southern Oregon when you started?

Audrey: No, I was through and I was working then in Medford but I spent every spare minute up there, after work at nights and all weekends I was there. It was so much fun and so rewarding not only to myself but everyone felt the same way.

STEDMAN AS CAPULET— An expert in stage construction and lighting, Stedman worked with Horace Robinson of University of Oregon in the production of the Trail to Rail Centennial in Klamath Falls.

Bob: We were doing other shows too at Southern Oregon so there were a lot of things going on at this time.

Audrey: I worked with Lois and Gus at the Normal School before they ever started the Festival. You see I went to the Normal in 1931 and 32 and I did a lot of backstage stuff in the play production for the school. Then it just naturally worked into the Festival.

Carrol: Who handled the finances for the organization? Who handled the money?

Bob: There wasn't any at first. What we did, Gus, Lois and I were the only ones who were old enough to sign chits for everything. We would go down to Hardy's Hardware and that's where I bought everything and they were good enough to let us go.

Carrol: In other words, they let you go on credit until you were able to get the money from the sale of tickets.

Bob: They didn't know for sure whether there was going to be any money. I always feel that they did a real good job helping us. After the first festival, we had two or three hundred dollars and when we started to put it in the bag, Dr. Redford said that Gus was working for Southern Oregon College and that the money had to go in the general fund. But he said that the money would be there and next year when we needed it we could take the money out. But the trouble was that

193

something happened in football and they didn't have enough money so that money went into football so we started again with nothing. The next year we made quite a bit more than we had made and in the next years until we finished in 1939, every year was better and money started to build up. A group was formed and they separated their money from state funds and put it in the bank. When I was there we never did get money from anybody else. The money came from what we did. Now they get a lot of money from others. This year we read that Fred Meyer gave them $250,000.

Carrol: But you still continued to make homemade costumes? It seems like it would be a tremendous challenge to try to costume one play when there was nothing that you could go to the store and buy.

Bob: A store, Perrine's, had some World War 1 drawers and I had a pair of those and the entire five years I used those for tights. They were wonderful and never did bag ever. We dyed them.

Carrol: They must have been slightly warm with all those lights.

Bob: Oh they were but sometimes it was pretty cold so it worked out

Audrey: They would costume one show. When they did the next show they would take this one's hat and tights, and this one's jacket and mingle them to make costumes for another show. So they looked like the costumes were new.

Carrol: Where did you store all the stuff?

Audrey: Well, it was bad at first. It was just in big boxes. Gus had a clothesrack in the back of his classroom and they were strung out there but it wasn't good. Gus would use them in his lectures sometimes. He taught ordinary English classes as well as Shakespeare but he seemed to be very much a zealot on Shakespeare and would undertake challenges that to me would seem impossible.

Bob: We didn't know that you can't do that kind of stuff so we did it.

Carrol: Where did Bowmer go to school?

Bob: Gus went to Bellingham and then he went to the University of Washington. He was employed out of the University of Washington. He hadn't finished his masters yet. Andrew Jackson was his thesis for his masters. It was a play and then they did it.

Carrol: You both acted in the Shakesperian Festival, didn't you?

Audrey: No, I didn't do any acting. I was a curtain page and opened and closed the show and pulled the curtains. Now they don't have any. At that time, they had three sets of curtains; the main curtain, the inner below and the inner above.

Carrol: One of your first plays was in Klamath Falls?

Bob: Gus always wanted a troop so we trooped Merchant of Venice to Klamath Falls. The students at the high school told other kids for everyone to get a quarter to go to the show and they would get out of school. So everybody got out of school. Some of them even came to the show too. As the gals with their tights came in to open the show the kids whistled, barked or something else. And when I came in my tights and pumpkin hose they whooped and hollered. But within three minutes they settled down and from then on they really loved it. When it was over the night show was supposed to be just for adults but the kids came too even some who had seen the afternoon show and a lot of them came because of word of mouth. So I felt that if we could reach the kids with this, we certainly would reach people who were interested in this kind of thing.

Carrol: Bob, what were some of the early plays that you did?

Bob: Merchant of Venice, Twelfth Night, Taming of the Shrew,

Romeo and Juliet, As you like it. In Hamlet, I did four or five parts. We didn't have enough players so I opened Hamlet, then I ran out and changed costumes. I was the poisoner so I ran out and changed costumes again and that's the way we did it.

Carrol: Probably there were some early-on troops who helped sustain this rather weakling organization. By weakling, I mean financial weakling. Were there other people who made contributions in terms of acting or otherwise in the early stages here?

Bob: In acting there were quite a few. Then there were people such as Walter Leverette, Mrs. Egan, and a bunch of people like that who started to get a group together. Most of them were from Medford.

Audrey: A lot of people came down from Cornish in Washington for the acting experience.

Bob: You see everybody who wants to be an actor wants to do some Shakespeare and for a long time they would have a lot of places where they would have Shakespeare plays and if you wanted a part, you could pay a hundred dollars for a good part. If you only had fifty dollars you could get a lesser role. We didn't charge anybody so there were a lot of people who came to do the shows from other universities just for the experience.

Carrol: Let me go back to this. While you folks never did charge anyone for the acting parts like many of the other summer theater groups were charging, this enhanced your opportunity to have people who could act well.

Bob: Yes

Audrey: There are a lot of actors now that were there in the beginning who are now professionals such as Stacy Keatch in the movies and George Peppard on television.

Bob: There were four of us that started the group that directed it. They were Gus, Lois, Bill Cottrell and me.

Even this small group of dedicated optimists would hardly have predicted the eventual status of their efforts. It is best summarized in a feature article in Newsweek magazine on August 1, 1983:

"Up in the idyllic small city of Ashland, Oregon, just over the California border, the 48-year-old ancestor of all American Shakespearean Festival roars along.

"Set in a picture-book valley in the Siskiyou Mountains, served by only one small commercial airport in nearby Medford, Ashland doesn't suggest itself as the prototypical place to imbibe Shakespeare. Its audiences are worlds apart from Stratford or London. At about 7 o'clock on a performance night, trucks ease into parking lots, each with a gang of scrubbed youngsters in the back. Then comes a busload or two of church groups from Grants Pass or Klamath Falls, followed by backpackers from any of a hundred spectacular campsites

THE STEDMANS—Audrey and Bob in retirement after a career in teaching and as an officer in the U.S. Army Combat Engineers. Daughter Marali, Mrs. Bob Bastian, said that by the time she attended SOCS the Shakespearian Festival employed mostly professional actors.

nearby. An hour before the three theaters open their doors, pipes and drums sound; singers and dancers arrive in costumes vaguely Elizabethan. There are madrigals, hornpipes, a naughty ballad or two. a sword dance. By showtime a small parcel of rural Oregon has been transmitted into a theatrical wonderland. The level of performance at Ashland is high enough to draw visitors from considerable distances. But there is also a sense of pride in Ashland itself, an outreach from festival to town that gives this immensely appealing city 15,200 a graciousness that most festival-ridden communities are hard pressed to muster.

"Shakespeare arrived in Ashland in the person of Angus Bowmer, who taught English and drama in Southern Oregon State College. In 1935 he persuaded the school to produce two plays over a July weekend. The following year Bowmer took his budding festival out of the school's purview and into the arms of Ashland's obliging town fathers, who turned over a piece of parkland for an outdoor theater. A flamboyant visionary and the stuff of instant legend, Bowmer directed, starred in, promoted, raised money and, in short, hoisted the banners high for Shakespeare in Ashland. By the time of his death in 1979, he had seen to the rebuilding of the outdoor theater, whose half-timbered, balconied stage is modeled on designs from Shakespeare's time, had given his name to a second theater, a 601-seat indoor structure, and had inspired a third installation, the Black Swan, an intimate room for more modest entertainment.

Incidental foofaraw aside, what Ashland gives its visitors is high-powered theater. Since the Angus Bowmer and Black Swan were added to the complex, the repertory has outgrown its original Elizabethan proportions; the "summer" season likewise runs from late February to the end of October.

"Ashland finally pulled down a Tony this year for regional theater excellence, national recognition at last for what staunch Oregonians have known and treasured for nearly a half a century."

The last time I saw Angus Bowmer he was on the rostrum of the Oregon House of Representatives. A special morning session has been called to honor him. I stayed at my desk and did not crowd into the gathering of political notables who were seeking to share the lights of the television cameras. Perhaps I felt a little humble over my prophecy of 1939. Certainly Gus deserved the tribute for, among other reasons, the ability to inspire the loyalty and devotion of people like the Stedmans.

DR. BERNARD DALY
The Man Who Loved Lake County

The Lakeview Roundup used to be, and probably still is, more than just a display of horse and cowboy skills. It was a homecoming for former Lake County people and an open house for visitors. Ranchers, townspeople, and outsiders alike, met to exchange news, gossip and stories.

My first visit to the Roundup was in 1931. My knowledge of rodeo events was nil. What impressed me more was the people themselves whose genuine warm friendliness and open-faced honesty was so evident even to an outsider.

A second thing that was impressive was a statement made by an obviously informed and honest resident, that Lakeview had a higher percentage of college graduates than any city in Oregon. What could possibly have brought about this amazing situation in a remote cow town like Lakeview? Probably the work of one man · Dr. Bernard Daly.

"Doc Daly would drive forty miles with a horse and buggy just to doctor a sick squaw." This was a statement made by U. E. Reeder whose father established a blacksmith shop in Lakeview in 1887. The statement by Reeder is confirmed by an article in the Lakeview Examiner on January 8, 1920 following Dr. Daly's death: "Many were the fearful night rides he was called upon to make, and numerous instances are related where he seemed to be possessed by almost superhuman endurance during his younger days. No instance is known where he refused to answer a call although he might have just returned from a long and tiresome trip extending over several days and nights."

What sort of a man would this be with such dedication and determination? Why has this doctor's name become almost always connected with higher education rather than medicine? Assembling accurate information on a person whose name became a legend shortly after his death in 1920 is a difficult job. This is especially true when that person affected the lives of so many people in so many capacities. It is fortunate that Les Shaw, then editor of the Lakeview Examiner, undertook the task of gathering information on Dr. Bernard Daly. Shaw was well qualified to do the research because he knew and enjoyed the confidence of the Lake County people and had the capability to weigh the results of his research in an objective manner. His story titled "Bernard Daly, One Man's Contribution" was printed in the Centennial edition of the Lakeview Examiner published on July 4, 1976. Feeling that the story of this remarkable man should go beyond the borders of Lake County and should be preserved in a permanent binding, I asked permission to use the information Shaw assembled and wrote. This permission he graciously gave me.

Shaw wrote: "Bernard Daly was born in County Mayo, Ireland, February 17, 1858. He was five years of age when his parents moved to the United States in 1863 and he grew up in Alabama. In 1886 he graduated from Ohio Northern University at Ada, Ohio, then called Ohio State Normal University. The next year he completed the medical course at Louisville, Kentucky . . . It didn't take long to become a doctor in those days. There were no textbooks on heart transplants, bio-chemistry, antibiotics or radiology. (Author's note: nor computerized blood analysis.) The newly graduated doctor came directly to Lakeview in 1887."

Shaw tried in vain to find a reason that the young doctor would come to Lakeview. He wrote, "The writer has searched the scanty historical writings about Bernard Daly trying to learn why he chose Lakeview. Had he heard of this place from a friend or relative? Did he simply leave medical school and start in search of a small town in which to practice? . . . If so, he surely passed through scores of similar small towns. Perhaps he just started west and traveled until he ran out of money. He never told anyone why he chose Lakeview."

Dr. Daly's accomplishments and activities were such that even before his death his works had become a legend. Like many legends, they were almost unbelievable and of course in this age of professional specialization, certification and licensing, it would be impossible.

One of his accomplishments was to organize the Bank of Lakeview in 1898. Shaw thought Daly became a banker, not by choice but by necessity. O. K. Burrell, a former Lakeview teacher and later a University of Oregon professor, wrote in the Oregon Business Review: "In most of these early day banks, private bankers did not suddenly become bankers. It is quite probable bankers became bankers without planning to do so. In Lakview, for example, Bernard Daly was a pioneer doctor who early in his career found it profitable to lend his surplus funds to businessmen and ranchers at high interest rates. At some point friends and associates began to entrust their funds to his care, which is another way of saying he began to accept deposits. It is doubtful that Dr. Daly could have determined precisely the date on which banking operations began . . . The Bank of Lakeview merely continued the banking enterprise of Dr. Daly."

Like many bankers, he was not always loved for his work as finance manager but apparently his popularity remained high as he was elected to the State Legislature as Representative in 1893. In the years 1897-98-99, he served in the State Senate. In 1900 Daly was Oregon's democratic party nominee to congress but was unsuccessful, being defeated by Thomas H. Tongue of Washington County. Following this, he was elected Lake County Judge in 1902 and served 12

YOUNG DOCTOR BERNARD DALY—Opinionated, gruff, always single. He never told why he came to Lakeview.

years in that position. During this tenure Lake County finances came from the red to the black and the beautiful old courthouse was completed in 1909. The total cost was $45,000.

Can a doctor who is a banker and a politician also become a rancher? Daly did it. He organized and was the president of the Lake County Land and Livestock Company. The headquarters ranch was the 7T at Plush.

Bryant Williams, who is knowledgeable in the history of the livestock industry, said that the substantial fortune accumulated was more the result of livestock operations than from medical practice. Daly would finance partners with a herd of sheep who would range the animals northward toward Silver Lake and the Wagontire Mountain region. The partners would then share in the profits from the increase. According to Bryant, descendants of the Daly partners are still living in northern Lake County. At the time of Daly's death, the 7T ranch properties were considered to be about one-fourth of the assets of his estate.

Could a man who was a doctor, banker, politician and rancher also become a lawyer? As incredible as it seems, Bernard Daly could and did. An Oregonian article printed in 1939 and reported by Les Shaw said: "Dr. Daly began studying law at the age of fifty (about 1908). He took the state bar and passed in 1911. He was appointed circuit judge in the new judicial district in 1914 and served through 1917. He also served on the town council."

JUDGE BERNARD DALY—
"It is my earnest desire to help and assist the ambitious young men and women of my beloved Lake County."

Surely a man of such talent and public concern would be loved by everyone and become a near candidate for sainthood. "Not so," says editor Shaw. "His popularity was not universal. The new doctor was an opinionated man, he was a gruff individual, had little sense of humor, he was tight with a buck and never married." Shaw traced down many of the adverse stories circulated by the enemies of the doctor and found them to be without foundation.

Daly's concern for the victims of the terrible Silver Lake fire of 1894 has become a classic story in the history of medicine. Shaw wrote: "Often retold was his assistance to men, women and children who were injured on Christmas Eve. In an upstairs community hall a Christmas Eve program was underway with some 160 persons attending when the fire broke out. Forty persons died in the fire and another 36 were injured. Of the latter, three died during the next three months making the toll 43."

Ed O'Farrell rode all night and through much of Christmas Day bringing word to Dr. Daly. With Willard Duncan, the driver, Dr. Daly left at 5 p.m. for Silver Lake, traveling in a buggy. He arrived at his

LESLIE SHAW—Editor,
Lake County Examiner
Lakeview, Ore. 1947-76

destination 13 hours later at about 6 a.m. and began three days and nights helping Silver Lake physician W. M. Thomson care for the injured. None of the patients ever received a bill from Dr. Daly.

Although Daly was highly successful in medicine, finance and law, it is in connection with education that he is and will be best remembered. He had no children but was elected to the school board the second year after arriving in Lakeview. Irregardless of his other activities, he served on the board for 30 years until shortly before his death. He was also appointed on the Board of Regents of the Oregon Agricultural College at Corvallis.

His concern and devotion to education was not really fully known until after his death. Again Shaw wrote, "It was his long service plus a close friendship with a teacher, Miss Pearl Hall, that guided Daly to establish the Bernard Daly Educational Fund. He almost waited too long.

"Dr. Daly's will, by which he established the scholarship fund, was signed on December 27, 1919, just nine days before his death on January 5, 1920. He had become ill shortly before Christmas, and the Examiner of January 1, 1920, reported that "The condition of Dr. Bernard Daly, who was taken seriously ill two weeks ago, is gradually improving, although he is still quite sick.

"On Sunday morning, January 4, 1920, Dr. Daly was taken aboard the train at Lakeview to go to a San Francisco hospital. He was accompanied by Dr. Charles Leithead, Fred Reynolds and Miss Pearl Hall. He died aboard the train near Livermore, California, at 5:30 the next morning, Monday, January 5, 1920. Services were held the following Sunday morning at St. Patrick's Catholic Church, and that afternoon at the Antlers (Elks) Hall.

"The following week The Examiner reported numerous inquiries about the scholarships provided by the will. The executors explained that first the will would have to be probated, the estate appraised and settled before it would be known what could be done; and besides, it would take until fall before sufficient funds could accumulate for scholarships, since only the earnings from the invested principal could be used.

"It was to be June 1922, before the first scholarships were announced. Use of the funds was delayed by suit in federal court, brought by relatives of Dr. Daly who asked that the will be thrown out as to the educational benefits. On May 12, 1921, Judge Bean in Portland handed down a decision disallowing the relatives' claims, and giving the complainants six months to appeal.

"The Daly will provided that the directors of the Bank of Lakeview would be the trustees of the Educational Fund, with the addition of the presidents of two state colleges, the University of Oregon and the Oregon State Agricultural College."

The first year there were 31 applicants for scholarships of which 19 were granted, all on the basis of scholarship. There were graduates who applied from Warner Lake, Paisley, Silver Lake and Summer Lake, as well as from Lakeview.

By 1922 the trustees had determined that the corpus (principal amount available) was $624,000. In recent years, wise and fortunate investments, plus changes in investment laws which allowed more diversified investments, has allowed the corpus to increase probably not as much as college costs have increased but in 1975, 20 students were awarded the fund to finance 4 years in Oregon state supported colleges. Tests are now administered to assure fairness in the selection of scholarship recipients.

Did Pearl Hall, the teacher, influence Bernard Daly while on that fateful train ride to leave his fortune to finance education? Not on your life! It would take the long and carefully planned work of a mind trained in banking and law to devise such an effective and lasting will which read: "It is my earnest desire to help and assist worthy and ambitious young men and women of my beloved County of Lake to acquire a good education, so that they may be better fitted and qualified to ap-

204

preciate and help preserve the laws and constitution of this free country, defend its flag, and by their conduct as good citizens reflect honor on Lake County and the State of Oregon."

The example and success of the Bernard Daly Fund has led others in Lake County to make similar bequests. I believe the recent establishment of the Merle and Emma West scholarship fund in Klamath County was also influenced by the example.

For whatever reason the young native of Ireland came to Lake County, it was a lucky day for the people there, both present and future. The large monument in the Lakeview cemetery, and the offerings of flowers each year by former recipients of the Bernard Daly Fund, shows that he will not be forgotten by those he called "beloved."

SOURCES

Aikens, C. Melvin, and others, "The Far West." **Ancient Native Americans.** W. H. Freeman and Co., San Francisco, 1978.

Bedwell, Steven F., **Fort Rock Basin History and Environment,** University of Oregon Books, Eugene, Oregon, 1973.

Bordaz, Jacques, "First Tools of Mankind." Natural History Magazine. Jan., Feb., 1959.

Breithaupt, Marilyn, Unpublished diary of Sarah Amanda Welch Rightmier.

Cressman, Luther S., and collaborators, **Archaeological Researches in the Northern Great Basin**, Carnegie Institutions of Washington Publication. No. 538, 1942.

————, **Prehistory of the Far West. Homes of Vanished Peoples.** University of Utah Press, Salt Lake City, Utah, 1977.

Crotty, Helen K., "A Modoc County Site." **Messages From The Past,** Monograph XX, Institute of Archaeology, University of California, Los Angeles, 1981.

Curtin, Jeremiah, **Myths of the Modocs; Indian Legends of the Northwest.** Benjamin Blom, Inc., Publishers, New York, 1971.

Davis Emma Lou, and others, **Evaluation of Human Activities and Remains in the California Desert.** Great Basin Foundation, Riverside, California, 1980.

Faulk, Odie B., **The Modoc People.** Indian Tribal Series, Phoenix, Arizona, 1976.

Fisher, Don, "Ben Wright," Unpublished papers in Siskiyou County Museum.

Gatschet, Albert S., **The Klamath Indians of Southwestern Oregon.** Contribution to North American Ethnology, Vol. 2, 1890.

Helfrich, Devere, **Klamath Echoes,** No. 3, Vol. 15. Klamath County Historical Society, 1966-77.

Hibben, Frank, **The Lost Americans.** Thomas Y. Crowell, New York, 1972.

Howe, Carrol B., **Ancient Tribes of the Klamath Country.** Binford and Mort, Portland Oregon, 1968.

————, **Ancient Modocs of California and Oregon.** Binford and Mort, Portland, Oregon, 1979.

Jennings, Jesse D., **Ancient Native Americans.** W. H. Freeman Co., San Francisco, California, 1978.

Jewett, Stanley G., "Klamath Basin Wildlife Refuges." Wildlife Leaflet No. 238. U.S. Department of Interior, Chicago, Illinois, 1943.

Johnson, LeRoy, "The Klamath Basin Archaeological Project." Descriptive Proposal to the National Science Foundation from Oregon Museum of Natural History, Eugene, Oregon, June 1, 1970.

Kirk, Ruth, The Oldest Man in North America. Harcourt Brace Jovanovich, Inc., New York, 1974.

Kittleman, Lawrence, "Tephra." Scientific American, Vol. 241, No. 6, Pages 160-177.

Lemke, R. W., and others, "Geologic Setting of the Glacier Peak and Mazama Ash-bed Markers in West Central Montana." Geological Survey Bulletin 1395-H, U.S. Government Printing Office, Washington, D.C. 1975.

McPhee, John, "Annals of A Former World." New Yorker Magazine, October 20-27, 1980.

Murray, Keith A., **The Modocs and Their War.** The University of Oklahoma Press, Norman, Oklahoma, 1965.

Ogden, Peter Skene, **Snake Country Journal.** 1826-27. The Hudson's Bay Record Society, London, 1961.

Ray, Verne F., **Primitive Pragmatists.** University of Washington Press, Seattle, 1963.

Rice, David, The Windust Phase in Lower Snake River Region Prehistory. Report of Investigations No. 50, Washington State University, Pullman, Washington, 1972.

Stern, Theodore, **The Klamath Tribe; A People and Their Reservation.** University of Washington Press, Seattle, 1965.

Stone, Buena, Brixner and Howe, **Ninety Years of Klamath Schools.** Published privately, 1960.

Wheat, Joe Ben, **A Paleo-Indian Bison Kill; Avenues to Antiquity.** Scientific American, W. H. Freeman Co., San Francisco, 1976.

Wheeler, Sessions S., **The Black Rock Desert.** Caxton Printers, Caldwell, Idaho, 1979.

Wormington, H. M., **Ancient Man in North America.** Denver Museum of Natural History, 1957.

Information by Interview:

C. Melvin Aikens
Ronald Angus
Adah Brown
Dewey Dietz
Jim DeVore
George Elliott
Eugene Gjertsen
Gary Hathaway
Elizabeth Henderson
Seldon Kirk

Audrey McPherson
Ray Michels
Robert Odell
Van Landrum
Richard Poole
James Rodgers
Dick Reeder
U. E. Reeder
Steve Wallman
Maxine Peterson Sweetman

Oral History Tape Recordings - All recorded by the author

Harry Boivin
Isabelle Borgman
Ellen Clark
Alfred Collier
Andrew Collier
Dibbon Cook
Percy Dixon
George Flitcraft
Wren Frain
Elvine and Roy Gienger
Alice Geary Kilham
Jack Linman

J. Paul Matthews
Lyle McCormick
Ben Murphy
Donovan Nicol
Ida Momyer Odell
Charles Ogle
Doris and Calvin Peyton
Margaret Reed
Martha Smith
Audrey and Bob Stedman
Sam Walker